HOUDINI

A MUSICAL

HOU

A MUSICAL

D&NI

By MURIEL RUKEYSER

PARIS
PRESS
Ashfield, Massachusetts
2002

Library of Congress Cataloging-in-Publication Data
Rukeyser, Muriel, 1913–1980
Houdini: a musical / by Muriel Rukeyser.--1st ed.
p.   cm.
ISBN 1-930464-04-5--ISBN 1-930464-05-3 (pbk.)
1. Houdini, Harry, 1874–1926--Drama.   2. Escape artists--Drama.
3. Magicians--Drama.
I. Title.

PS3535.U4 H68 2002
812'.52--dc21

2002070378

TP 1-930464-05-3
TC 1-930464-04-5

First Edition.

A C E G I J H F D B

Printed in the United States of America.

Paris Press dedicates *Houdini*
to the memory of Monica McCall

A NOTE FROM THE PUBLISHER

In 1973, Lyn Austin produced *Houdini: A Musical* at the Lenox Center for the Performing Arts in Lenox, Massachusetts. Christopher Walken played Houdini; Grover Dale was the director; and David Spangler composed the music. *Houdini* received favorable reviews in the *New York Times* and regionally, but it was never produced again and never published. It is a privilege for Paris Press to bring this celebration of two remarkable human beings—Muriel Rukeyser and Harry Houdini—into the world.

At the beginning of *Houdini,* Rukeyser's character Marco Bone tells us that the musical is part biography, part fantasy. The verse drama unlocks many mysteries for those who are unfamiliar with Houdini's life, and it invites us all to contemplate the metaphors of locks, keys, escape—and the body, a theme that is unquestionably shared by Rukeyser the poet and Harry Houdini the illusionist. "I speak through the body," says Houdini in response to questioning during the anti-fortune telling congressional hearings of 1926 (p. 126).

Desire, love, and searching—other recurrent Rukeyser themes—are present in this verse drama as well. So are fear and the will to overcome fear, issues that Houdini faced as he continually put himself into life-threatening situations and overcame the danger of those situations.

Who, in *Houdini,* is the escape artist or the illusionist? Is it the writer, the magician, or the reader? Rukeyser anchors us, sharpening our ability to see and to feel. What parts of our lives are simultaneously real and unreal, truth and fantasy? And how does that extend to politics and deception, to the details of daily living, to hope and loyalty, and to the most dangerous feats of strength and endurance?

Muriel Rukeyser worked on *Houdini* for decades before the musical debuted. One of the most famous lines from her poetry, taken up again and again by the women's movement, is spoken by Houdini's wife Bess: "What would happen if one woman told the truth about her life? The world would split open." And here Houdini answers: "It has. Now I'm going after it—all pieces." Then he sings "I Make My Magic" (p. 89).

Rukeyser researched Houdini's life, using the information that was available to her at the time. Occasionally, events are portrayed which have since been rejected as untrue (compare one of her sources, *Houdini: His Life Story* by Arnold Kellock, 1928, with the recent definitive biography *Houdini!!!* by Kenneth Silverman, 1996). One instance occurs when Houdini first meets Bess, spills acid on her dress, and then asks his mother to re-create the piece of clothing. As metaphorical as this sounds, the event Rukeyser portrays is included as fact in Kellock's biography. In contrast, Rukeyser also includes portions of Houdini's actual testimony against spiritualism, which took place during the anti-fortune telling hearings. In a note to the director Rukeyser says: "This seems to go off into the absurd here. However, almost all of this scene is taken from the transcript of the actual hearing." She does, however, opt to change several names.

Muriel Rukeyser willed *Houdini* to her longtime companion and agent, Monica McCall, along with a coral necklace and her topaz ring. Among Rukeyser's papers are documents indicating that McCall worked closely with Rukeyser during the Lenox production. On McCall's letterhead is a hand-written note marked "RE: HOUDINI" that says: "Frame of investigation—persecuting ourselves into truth. The magic is in the waking." And then it quotes Marilyn Monroe: " 'If you want your dream to come true, you have to wake up.' "

The text of *Houdini* follows Muriel Rukeyser's manuscript, which she completed in 1973, after the Lenox production. In preparing *Houdini* for publication, Paris Press editorially and ty-pographically replicated Rukeyser's style as closely as possible, while making consistent character names and spelling through-out the work. David Spangler helped to provide Paris Press with several lyrics that were referred to in the text and in the front matter of the musical, but were missing from the body of the manuscript.

I thank Catherine Graham for allowing Paris Press to publish *Houdini.* I thank Marc Comras for his advice and expertise, Anne Goldstein for her tenacious and bountiful editorial assis-tance, and Jeff Flannery from the Library of Congress, Kristin Bengston, Jenna Evans, Tzivia Gover, Diane Edington, Mary Lucas, Martin Moran, and Nancy Freeman for their help in the early stages of research and production. Thank you, Terry Nemeth and Kathy Sova for production advice, Ivan Holmes and Susan Gerber for beautiful design and typesetting, and a sky full of thanks to David Spangler for feedback, enthusiasm, and gener-ous assistance. I thank the National Endowment for the Arts, the Massachusetts Cultural Council, and many benevolent individu-als for helping Paris Press publish this work.

Finally, thank you to Sidney H. Radner for his comments and support, and for his generosity in offering Paris Press the cover art for the book. Sidney Radner's expertise about Houdini has been inspiring, and I am grateful for his lifetime dedication to Harry Houdini and for his determination to carry to the public a greater understanding of this fascinating and courageous man.

— JAN FREEMAN

HOUDINI

A MUSICAL

By MURIEL RUKEYSER

The play is in two acts. The time is the legendary past of circuses, carnivals, and magic acts. Historically, the first quarter of the twentieth century, slides to the present time.

ACT ONE

ACT TWO

No time passes between ACTS ONE *and* TWO, *except, of course, for the audience.*

CHARACTERS
(in order of their appearance)

HOUDINI – *Harry Houdini, born Ehrich Weiss*
BEATRICE – *his wife, also known as* BESS
MARCO BONE – *the magician's assistant*
CECILIA WEISS – *Houdini's mother*
KIVIE GRATTAN – *the circus man*
MRS. MURPHY – *a gun juggler*
EPICTETUS – *a clown*
WHITSUN – *a clown*
JUDY – *a circus woman*
VOLONTY – *star of the circus, a high-wire dancer who also tells fortunes; she is Black.*
WARDEN
PRISONER IN SOLITARY – *he is Black.*
SIR ARTHUR CONAN DOYLE
LADY DOYLE
MR. HOLMES
THREE MEDICAL STUDENTS
MEDIUMS, CONEY ISLAND PEOPLE, REPORTERS, PEOPLE WITH CHAINS, CONGRESSMEN, FORTUNE-TELLERS . . .

SONGS, DANCE, AND MUSICAL NUMBERS

ACT ONE
Scene One

"Coney Island"........................ENSEMBLE
"Let Me See, Let Me Feel".......HOUDINI, BEATRICE
"Rosabelle"..................HOUDINI, BEATRICE
"Yes"....................MARCO BONE, BEATRICE
Ribbon Tap-Dance............ENSEMBLE, HOUDINI

Scene Two

"You Don't Know What You're Missing"...ENSEMBLE
"Chow"....................WHITSUN, EPICTETUS
"Beer and Bacon".........................VOLONTY
"Nickels and Dimes"..........HOUDINI, BEATRICE, VOLONTY, MARCO BONE
Borneo Dance........HOUDINI, ENSEMBLE, VOLONTY, BEATRICE

Scene Three

"Hostility"............BLACK PRISONER, PRISONERS

Scene Four

River Music
"Chains, Freedom, Keys"..................HOUDINI
"In the Dark, in the Deep Dark".. HOUDINI, ENSEMBLE

ACT TWO
Scene One

"The Mediums"........................ENSEMBLE
"I Make My Magic"......................HOUDINI

Scene Two

"What the King Said"........MARCO BONE, BEATRICE
Séance Music
"Floating Figures".....................ENSEMBLE
"When Mr. Holmes Goes Into His Dance".. SHERLOCK
HOLMES, VOLONTY
"Beatrice's Song Cycle".........BEATRICE, HOUDINI,
VOLONTY, MARCO BONE, ENSEMBLE

Scene Three

"Ecstasy of a Woman Detective"...........VOLONTY
"Let Me See, Let Me Feel"................HOUDINI

ACT ONE

ACT ONE, SCENE ONE

The stage is a box of night. A curtain across the back of the stage, half scarlet, light coursing upward, half with a cascade of light down blue-green—a reminder of rivers, dreamlike states of being, whatever water-movement gives you.

In the middle of the stage, HOUDINI *the young man, intense physically and emotionally splendid, concentrated and braced, chest spread.*

Immediately, the ENSEMBLE *begins to form across the stage and in front of* HOUDINI. *They carry doors of color. They merge around these doors and block* HOUDINI *with a transparent door, gleaming like water.*

ENSEMBLE
    I see a man. I cannot see his eyes—
    I see a woman putting on a ring—
    I see a gold key. I see a gold key—
    I see fire. I see fire. It looks like hell—
    Or is it . . . the foundation . . .
    Of something?

(HOUDINI *pushes the door open with a great swimming movement. The* ENSEMBLE *is frozen around him. He looks at us with his compelling, light-filled eyes.*)

HOUDINI

My mind is open. I want to believe, but nothing I have ever seen or heard, so far, can convince or prove to me . . .
(He is a showman; however, here he is speaking from his own self, he believes what he says.

MARCO BONE, *the Magician's Assistant, echoes it from* HOUDINI's *shoulder. He is tall, saturnine, essential to* HOUDINI *for many reasons. He announces the turns of* HOUDINI's *life, and it is clear soon that* MARCO BONE *is not a magician.*)

MARCO BONE

Convince or prove to me . . .

HOUDINI and MARCO BONE

Convince or prove to me . . .
Convince or prove to me . . .
(The ENSEMBLE, *defeated, moves away with their doors. The lights course down the curtain and across the floor, the upward lights across the ceiling, and then disappear.*

HOUDINI *is strengthening himself as* MARCO BONE *begins to speak. He makes shapes on the air. He is the contortionist; he deepens his breathing; a current of energy begins in his right hand, travels up his right arm; his left hand begins; quickly, his whole body is involved.*)

MARCO BONE

Tonight, ladies and gentlemen, we are privileged to see the man who can melt chains, melt bracelets, defy the bricked-up wall, the most spectacular of them all. He is no stranger to any of you. He's a myth. But he's sound. American as hamburger. American, like the Bible. Help me, music.

I believe in the future of Houdini. He's my immortality, he's my business. Don't let me sell you anything. I'm praising him ahead of time. He's here! . . .
(HOUDINI *juggles rhythms on his empty arms.*)
I'm Marco Bone and I can tell you your name.
I've got tricks in my knuckles, sometimes, like
anyone. Your drums, boys, and the hurry-hurry-hurry!
He remembers beginnings. Hours. Circuses.
A butterfly in Wisconsin. How his birthday was
turned into a lock. What happened, Harry?
(*The boy* HOUDINI *is practicing with a rope-end.*)

HOUDINI

The promise.

MARCO BONE

He was twelve and he knew one thing . . .

HOUDINI

Two things.

MARCO BONE

He knew locks, and what else?

5

HOUDINI
How to pick up needles with my eyelids.

MARCO BONE
(*The boy is running.*)
It's his birthday. His father calls him in, and says, "Ehrich," (the boy was born Ehrich Weiss) "promise me something."

HOUDINI
(*In a very young voice.*)
Yes, father, what?

MARCO BONE
His father was old and religious. His mother was young and beautiful. His father never got used to anything: not America, or speaking English, or raising money for the temple. He's a rabbi. Maybe God, he's used to. He's a progressive, yes, but he lives by proverbs, and they tell him it's a sin to be a magician . . .

HOUDINI
What, father?

MARCO BONE
(*Taking on the character of* HOUDINI's *father.*)
Your mother—

HOUDINI
(*Complex feeling and pressure in his body and voice.*)
Something about mother?

MARCO BONE
> (As HOUDINI's *father.*)
> You would do anything for her?

HOUDINI
> Yes.

MARCO BONE
> Say after me, I swear,

HOUDINI
> I swear —

MARCO BONE
> That I will —

HOUDINI
> That I will —

MARCO BONE
> Take care of —

HOUDINI
> Take care of —

MARCO BONE
> Mother —

HOUDINI
> Mother —

MARCO BONE
> She must not come —

HOUDINI
She must not come —

MARCO BONE
— to want.

HOUDINI
— to want.
(This is the key, this word. Music.)

MARCO BONE
You're a good boy, Ehrich. I'm old. I'm old.

ENSEMBLE
You don't look old.

MARCO BONE
I'm not his father. I'm Marco Bone, and this is a free fantasy on the situation of Houdini. It's an American myth of the escape artist, a play of people fiercely involved in magic, denial, extreme physical life, attempts at communication, and the juggling of images of themselves. It is made in continual transformations, beginning with Coney Island. He is nineteen now, and doing a magic act in a high school, playing with acid.
(This statement announces the transformations of our play, and wards off any charges that it is biographical. It allows for MARCO BONE'S *sense of wonder. It invites the* ENSEMBLE *to reappear as Coney Island people, here at the school where young* HOUDINI *is performing as a fledgling. For we are coming to the first day of his life as a magician — what he wants to be, what he must be, with the drive behind every drop of his blood.)*

ENSEMBLE   *(Song: "Coney Island")*
CONEY ISLAND, CONEY ISLAND,
NO NEED TO LET ME KNOW,
NO NEED TO TELL ME SO
I NEED YOU NOW TO SHOW ME . . .
(HOUDINI spills acid on BEATRICE's dress, as she sits in the front row. He tears off the dress. They meet.

The sound that goes with the spilling of the acid is a key sound that will be developed throughout the show. We see BEATRICE as HOUDINI does, young, soft, spotlit, all the strength and imagination ready to emerge, but sheltered, protected now, too protected. The burning is the initiation.)

HOUDINI and BEATRICE   *(Song: "Let Me See, Let Me Feel")*
LET ME SEE,
LET ME FEEL,
LET ME KNOW WHAT IS REAL,
LET ME BELIEVE.

MARCO BONE
He's bringing the dress home to his mother.

HOUDINI
What's that, mother?

MARCO BONE
I'm stretching the meat.

HOUDINI
Could you copy this dress?
(A dress of a special pink.)

9

MARCO BONE

A girl? Ehrich, you? The eggshell is still on you.

HOUDINI

You'll make the dress, won't you?

MARCO BONE

She'll make the dress. Pink and new. Perfect. Now she is giving him the dress. Softly, gently, she cries.

ENSEMBLE

You're not crying.

MARCO BONE

I'm not his mother.

ENSEMBLE   *(Song: "Coney Island" continued)*
SHOW ME WHAT'S UNDER THE COUNTER,
SHOW ME WHAT'S UNDER YOUR SKIN,
SHOW ME THE WAY TO GET OUT
AND I'LL SHOW YOU THE WAY TO GET IN.

SHOW ME LIFE, SHOW ME LIVES, PEOPLE IN DIVES,
SHOW ME YELLS, SHOW ME SMELLS, AND GRIMY HOTELS,
CLAMS, YAMS, LOBSTER AND SHRIMPS,
SAND, CANDY, PANDERS AND PIMPS,
SHOW ME BIM, SHOW ME BAM, BAMBOOZLE ME,
BOOZE ME AND USE ME AND FOOZLE ME,
SHOW ME RIDES, SHOW ME SLIDES, PEOPLE IN TIDES,
SHOW ME MONEY, SHOW ME FUNNY, SHOW ME THE SEA,
YOU, SHOW, ME.

(The ENSEMBLE *is now the Coney Island people: a* CHORUS
GIRL, *a* SAILOR, *a* FAT MAN, *a* NURSE *crying "Shame!" and
"Don't touch it!" to an invisible little boy she is chasing. It is
the bright-colored world of touch and live to* HOUDINI, *and
the opening of the whole world to* BEATRICE.

HOUDINI *and* BEATRICE *enter. She is wearing the pink dress
as she comes into her new world; the protected and demure
girl, but ready for whatever comes next with* HOUDINI. *He is
callow, unformed, a young fellow with a job, moonlighting
with card tricks and clumsy attempts. He wears a gray suit
and a loud tie. They are on the boardwalk, deep in talk.)*

HOUDINI
Don't you believe me?

BEATRICE
That's a lot to ask on the first date.
*(She advances and withdraws, that is her movement. They
reach the rail.)*
Harry Houdini, there's the whole sea!
Clams. Seashells. Wax paper.
Beer. Burnt metal.
Fry fat. Tar.

HOUDINI
Anything else?

BEATRICE
Pee pee.

11

HOUDINI
You're a little kid.

BEATRICE
Your voice shakes, and you're a grown man.

HOUDINI
(She does know, already, and he can speak to that.)
When did you know?

BEATRICE
When the acid spilled. Mother wanted you put in jail.

HOUDINI
The burn ran down your dress.
(He allows it its sexual meaning.)

BEATRICE
Would it have hurt me?

HOUDINI
(He does not answer directly.)
Let's go down.
(They jump down to the sand. We see the dark under the board-walk, the lovers under there; people changing their clothes.)

BEATRICE
I've never been anywhere.

HOUDINI
We'll go everywhere there is. You know, I'm still stuck in that necktie factory.

(Cries, some near, some very faint: Shame! Shame! . . . Come find me! I'm not lost!—Music from a faraway carousel.)
That's the song when the acid spilled!
(They laugh. He picks up the song. He sings in a strange voice.)

HOUDINI and BEATRICE   *(Song: "Rosabelle")*

HOUDINI

> ROSABELLE, MY ROSABELLE,
> I LOVE YOU MORE THAN I CAN TELL—

Come on, sing after me:

> OVER ME YOU CAST A SPELL—

BEATRICE

> OVER ME YOU CAST A SPELL—

HOUDINI

> I LOVE YOU, MY SWEET ROSABELLE,

BEATRICE

> I LOVE YOU, MY SWEET . . .

(She fades out.)
Why do they make me stay away from here?
Away from theater? Away from anything?
(She bursts out.)
Fifty Hail Mary's . . .

HOUDINI

I may be working here.

BEATRICE

Coney Island?

13

HOUDINI
Your voice is beautiful.

BEATRICE
You're really at home here, aren't you?

HOUDINI
(He holds out his hand. A movement travels from it into his body.)
It's a kind of tremor, but I mustn't tremble.
It's my chance here. I have to see what I can really do.

BEATRICE
You do magic.

HOUDINI
— Not really magic.

BEATRICE
Don't shield me. I'm not a child.

HOUDINI
(Juggles nothing in two rhythms on his two arms.)
Bim. Bam. Boozle. Got it. What do you want it to be?

BEATRICE
A burning star. Like you.

HOUDINI
There's nothing there. Just some fast finger work. You like my tricks, don't you?

BEATRICE
They make me afraid.

HOUDINI

Control that. That's what I do. I have to control my fear, and every muscle in my body. I train my hands, my fingers, my thumbs, my . . .

BEATRICE

What fear?

HOUDINI

A promise I made when I was twelve, to take care of someone. I ran away. How do you find money, if all you know is how to pick up needles with your eyelids?

BEATRICE

You knew locks. You know fear. You can go anywhere with that.

HOUDINI

(*Looks at her narrowly, suddenly seeing all that she has for him.*)
I know locks. A lock is a . . . lake, and I want to swim through it. I'd like to be in the ocean, with you. Come under the boardwalk.

BEATRICE

(*She will not answer that.*)
How do you pick up needles with your eyelids?

HOUDINI

(*Intently, as if he were describing sex.*)
You place a needle on a plain piece of paper. You stare straight at it. You don't move your eyes until the needle is all you see.

Then slowly you lower your head towards it. It blurs out into a gray shape and your eyelashes just touch the paper. You begin to close your eyelids until they touch the needle. You control your muscles. And you control your fear. Now you know all.

BEATRICE

You could do anything.
(The people on the beach are still for a moment.)
Look—they're stones, they're statues of themselves.
You can see what they need.
Look—we could have a mind-reading act.
Harry—if you bend over me, they'll think we're kissing.
Look—if you could stand up now and say to them:
"My fear—look what I do with it!"

HOUDINI

When I touch you I know.

BEATRICE

Somebody like you—you could lead them along.

HOUDINI

(A change of mood. Jubilant.)
Now you're in my act!
Sign an agreement: lifetime secrecy.
We'll be famous. I love you!
(He moves toward her, loses focus as if she were the needle. He kisses her, fiercely.)

BEATRICE

Yes.
(She answers before the question.)

HOUDINI

Don't cry . . . Yes, cry.
(*He somehow allows, somehow wants, her tears.*)
Will you be punished?

BEATRICE

That's the least of it.

HOUDINI

If you were mine, I wouldn't let them punish you. I'm going to get a job here.
(MARCO BONE *appears, with a stamp of his tall pole, speaking to them.*)

MARCO BONE

Interesting here, ain't it. Plenty to do for two. Lots of ways to do it.

HOUDINI

And here's Marco. Marco!

MARCO BONE

It begins with a "B" . . . Bess.
Yes, Bess, in her dress.
Better than new.

HOUDINI

I'm going to see the big boss.
Going to try for that job.

BEATRICE

Don't leave me.

HOUDINI
    (Turning away.)
    Don't terrify the lady, Marco.
    (The shooting gallery appears: a long, horizontal row of targets, curious emblems painted on them.)

MARCO BONE
    Not for the world, my dear.
    (Exit HOUDINI. BEATRICE *goes with* MARCO BONE *to the shooting gallery, and a crowd gathers round.)*
    Try your hand, try your hand!
    Some are easy, some are hard.
    Here's the key to your first house; the hand
    of Mozart; the cloud-by-day, to lead you across
    the desert; the mirror you know so well.
    Here's the left breast of Cleopatra, and Antony's cock.
    *(BEATRICE *shoots at the first target when* MARCO BONE *gives her a pole to shoot with; then she gives the gun to the* SAILOR, *who hits all the targets. The last one shoots back at him.)*

MARCO BONE
    (To BEATRICE.*)*
    You're in the country of the targets. And the guns, too, of course. What do you get when a gun marries a target?

BEATRICE
    A clarinet? A congressman?
    (She passes the test; he likes her fantasy, and begins to accept her.)

MARCO BONE
    You like Harry's act, don't you?
    Obviously.

(BEATRICE *is being led into her new life. During this song, she realizes it fully. Still wary of each other,* MARCO BONE *and* BEATRICE *both love* HOUDINI, *and they recognize it and the other.*)

MARCO BONE and BEATRICE   *(Song: "Yes")*

MARCO BONE

       IT'S LIKE A TAP-DANCE
       OR A NEW PINK DRESS,
       A SHIT-NAIVE FEELING,
       SAYING YES.

       SOME SAY GOOD MORNING
       SOME SAY GOD BLESS—
       SOME SAY POSSIBLY
       SOME SAY YES.

       SOME SAY NEVER
       SOME SAY UNLESS
       IT'S STUPID AND LOVELY
       TO RUSH INTO YES.

       WHAT CAN IT MEAN?
       IT'S JUST LIKE LIFE,
       ONE THING TO YOU
       ONE TO YOUR WIFE.

       SOME GO LOCAL
       SOME GO EXPRESS
       SOME CAN'T WAIT
       TO ANSWER YES.

SOME COMPLAIN
OF STRAIN AND STRESS
THEIR ANSWER MAY BE
NO FOR YES.

SOME LIKE FAILURE
SOME LIKE SUCCESS
SOME LIKE YES YES
YES YES YES.

OPEN YOUR EYES,
DREAM BUT DON'T GUESS.
YOUR BIGGEST SURPRISE
COMES AFTER YES.

(MARCO BONE *and* BEATRICE *sing three verses. They con-clude:*)

YOUR BIGGEST SURPRISE,
YOUR BIGGEST SURPRISE
COMES AFTER . . .
COMES AFTER . . .

(Enter HOUDINI.*)*

HOUDINI

I got the job. No more neckties.
(He produces a pair of scissors and cuts his tie off.)
Let's get . . .

BEATRICE

(Not letting him say it.)
. . . married!

HOUDINI

(He catches his breath, but he likes it.)

Yes.

(The Ribbon Tap-Dance, to the music of "Yes," with long, colored streamers as the whole ENSEMBLE *dances. One brings in a glass and cloth, the one remnant of the Jewish wedding. On the last note of the dance,* HOUDINI *stamps on the glass triumphantly. It shatters.*

ENSEMBLE *sings three verses of "Yes." All exit but* MARCO BONE. *He reports on the wedding and the homecoming, speaking again directly to the audience.)*

MARCO BONE

Yes, I was the best man.

They were married by Boss McKane,

he gave Harry his job that afternoon

and gave his blessing to Bess and the boy that night.

Sure, nobody cried.

The whole thing happened in royal humor . . .

Sure, he took her home to mother . . .

Sure, Cecilia takes in roomers . . .

Sure, she governs the traffic . . .

Sure, Harry was sent to bed alone . . .

Sure, Bess has just stopped crying.

Alone on the thinnest mattress,

on the floor of the passageway across the hall.

Skinnier than anyone, that mattress is, except Bone.

Does marriage change the color of things? Yes.

I wouldn't let anybody separate me.

But then I'm a divorced man.

(HOUDINI *enters* BEATRICE's *room. Long embrace. One pillow on the little bed.*)

HOUDINI
We'll go to a hotel tomorrow.
Here . . . sign this.
What's the time?

BEATRICE
I don't know.

VOICES
10:20 P.M.

HOUDINI
Thank you. What are you doing?

BEATRICE
Reading it.

HOUDINI
Don't you trust me?

BEATRICE
It's a diagram, your family tree? . . .

HOUDINI
You like it?

BEATRICE
Your mother's on one side of you.
I'm on the other . . .
Harry Houdini, it's a burial plot!

HOUDINI
Stay with me always . . . a lasting proof.

BEATRICE
I gave you proof today. I married you.

HOUDINI
Sign it. I need it!
(She signs. HOUDINI *takes the pen, writes a short note, and
pins it to the pillow.)*
For the morning. It tells you everything.

BEATRICE
Tell me now.

HOUDINI
I'll be up and gone at six. The note will tell you.

BEATRICE
Where will you be?

HOUDINI
Mother wakes me in time for two hours of exercise and study
every day. Training. You know, bim, bam, boozle . . .

BEATRICE
Fingers of fire. The blazing man.

HOUDINI
(He takes the black bandage from his sleeve.)
With a trick up his sleeve.

BEATRICE

What are you doing?

HOUDINI

Putting on my night eyes.
(Mysterious voice.)
I like my night eyes.
What would you want, in the whole world, Bess?

BEATRICE

Anything you want. You know what I'd love?
I'd love to be in your acts with you . . . if you like.
You are everything; standing on a mountain,
streaming fire from your hands and feet . . .

HOUDINI

And my head and my sex, streaming fire and sperm, in perfect
control . . .

BEATRICE

Yes, and everyone watching.
I watch too, all our faces . . .
*(She wipes her forehead with her hand. Their whole bodies
are engaged. It is herself she is describing.)*

HOUDINI

Gleaming.

BEATRICE

Gleaming . . .
Their eyes open as never before.

HOUDINI
My eyes closed as never before. Touching.

BEATRICE
We are all watching you.

HOUDINI
And I am touching . . .
　　　　　. . . yes!
(The MAGIC. BEATRICE *is lying on the pillow with* HOUDINI.
She rouses into her dream or fantasy. She lifts her arms;
HOUDINI *enters her fantasy. He goes to the center of the*
stage and speaks.)
More than mountains, higher than the high clouds,
We begin, locked together,
Further than man has ever flown,
Traveling freely in free fall, love,
Flying with all the powers,
Discovering each other, our long dance
Down the air, down the hours,
Deep into our lives. Our life.
Flying fuck.
Discovery, discovery.
(He goes back to her on the pillow. They sleep.

A knock on the door. A face at the window. HOUDINI *is called
to his morning. He rouses and exits.*

BEATRICE *wakes to see the great face of* CECILIA *over her. It
is a mask face on a woman's body. The face is strong and
haunting, but it is basically the face of* BEATRICE, *older, with
the hypnotic eyes of* HOUDINI. *The woman's body under it is*

young and voluptuous, fuller than the body of BEATRICE, *but the same height. The* ENSEMBLE, *or five members of the* ENSEMBLE, *is/are the voice of* CECILIA. *Her color is the pink we know.)*

ENSEMBLE *(As* CECILIA*)*
(The household indoctrination.)
Two hours now for his joints and muscles.
Two hours later for his books . . .

BEATRICE
. . . muscles . . .

ENSEMBLE
Two hours later in the magic stores.
He buys his tricks.
Someday, he'll invent them all.

BEATRICE
. . . magic . . .

ENSEMBLE
Then, his shirts must be done *just so* . . .

BEATRICE
. . . magic . . .

ENSEMBLE
. . . Not too much starch, but a little . . .

BEATRICE
. . . magic . . .

ENSEMBLE
> . . . Check all the buttons . . .

BEATRICE
> . . . muscles . . .

ENSEMBLE
> . . . When there are French cuffs, put out the cuff links . . .

BEATRICE
> . . . magic muscles . . .

ENSEMBLE
> . . . He has only one shirt with French cuffs just now . . . He
> plans his time to the minute . . .

BEATRICE
> . . . Thank you.

ENSEMBLE
> . . . He's very aware of time . . .

BEATRICE
> . . . time . . .

ENSEMBLE
> . . . You'll keep the clock wound . . .

BEATRICE
> . . . magic . . . time . . .

ENSEMBLE

. . . He waits, and drills his body.
He's really a man of ritual.
You'll see.

BEATRICE

. . . man . . . ritual . . . man . . .
(*Exit* CECILIA. BEATRICE *reads the note on the pillow.*)
"My Bess, you give me my real life. Behind my night eyes I
see you. I need you looking at me. Thank you for the way
you are with her. Tonight we'll go to a hotel. I love you."

ACT ONE, SCENE TWO

The HOUDINIs *arrive at a circus in New England on a rainy Sunday night. The circus is bankrupt. Some of its people are in jail for breaking the blue laws that say no performances on Sunday. The circus performers who are left are highly colored, desperate, going on because there is nothing else. They see uses for* HOUDINI *when he is able to get out of a locked trunk, and uses for* BEATRICE *when she says she will do anything for her husband—they need a lot of singing and stealing.*

GRATTAN, *the circus man, leads* HOUDINI *to the jail, where he is able to free the others, chiefly* VOLONTY, *the high-wire artist and fortune-teller. Back at the circus,* HOUDINI *makes a deal that includes hiring* MARCO BONE. *The circus pulls out.*

ENSEMBLE   *(Song: "You Don't Know What You're Missing")*
          YOU DON'T KNOW WHAT YOU'RE MISSING
          IF YOU'RE MISSING THE CIRCUS TONIGHT
          YOU DON'T KNOW WHAT YOU'RE MISSING
          IF YOU'RE MISSING THE CIRCUS TONIGHT
          YOU DON'T KNOW WHAT YOU DON'T KNOW
          IF YOU HAVEN'T SEEN THE WHOLE SHOW
          AT THE CIRCUS TONIGHT . . .

(The ENSEMBLE *is circus people. This is* GRATTAN*'s circus on a bad night in New England. Heavy rain, the sound of a train whistle fairly near, and then diminishing. A few people standing around and getting supper: a* SPANISH DANCER, THREE CLOWNS, MRS. MURPHY *the gun-juggler,* GRATTAN, *a gambling man at a low point. He is a big man, an exaggeration in everything he does. Around them the worn, glorious red-and-gold of the shabby circus. At one side, a roaring tiger-face, its mouth open as big as a door. A big, brass-bound trunk, center foreground.)*

GRATTAN
    My god, how much rain can there be?
    There are fish in the mousetraps.
    Who'll go to the circus?
    Only Noah will be left, and he has his own . . .
    Anybody get here?

ENSEMBLE
    (They are standing in the entrance.)
    Only the Houdinis.

GRATTAN
    Where's Fritz with the money?
    Well, good, the Houdinis.

BILL
    What can they do?

HOUDINI
    Anything.

GRATTAN
   When do we eat?

WHITSUN and EPICTETUS
   Inter, mitzy, titsy, tool
   Alabama Dominoo,
   Ocracoker, Dominoker,
   Two minutes, boss . . .

GRATTAN
   Where's chow?

WHITSUN
   Go down the road and pick up something.

BILL
   You see anything?

WHITSUN
   One house all dark in the evening. Big kitchen.
   And a meat market with a cat sitting in the window.
   And some good windows that were partly open.

GRATTAN
   (Ferociously.)
   Just get it back here soon.
   (Exit WHITSUN *and* EPICTETUS.*)*
   Have a chair, Mrs. Houdini. Here's how we'll do it. First the
   sideshow. Ever done fortune-telling? Well, Volonty will break
   you in. In the tent, Houdini to do magic, what I saw you do
   at Tony Pastor's, only more of it. Stretch it.

MRS. MURPHY

Well, hand over your clothes, you two. I'll hang them up. Can you let them have a towel, Pud?

PUD

Sure. Just for now.

GRATTAN

And the handcuff act. But not refined. Lots of bracelets. Let them come out of the audience and snap them on your arms — if they've bought a ticket to the sideshow.

MRS. MURPHY

What sideshow?

GRATTAN

Oh, a month from now! Freaks . . . And of course, you both are in the parade. Twenty-five a week and cakes. Everything satisfactory?

BEATRICE

Mr. Grattan, what's cakes?

GRATTAN

Never been under the canvas, hey? If I had a wife, that's the . . . second thing she'd know. Cakes, that's grub, such as it is, chow — what we're waiting for now. Whitsun? How about it?

WHITSUN

Are we sending some down to the girls?

GRATTAN
Some of our people are having steak with the sheriff.

WHITSUN and EPICTETUS   *(Song: "Chow")*
(Back with the food.)
        CHOW FOR MY MOUTH
        CHILI FROM THE SOUTH
        BEANS FROM THE EAST
        MEAT FROM THE WEST
        ICE CREAM, NORTH —
        DRINK FROM THE RYE,
        WATER FROM THE SKY —
        I LIVE HIGH!
(They gather around.)

GRATTAN
Here are the new ones, the Houdinis, Harry and Bess.

MRS. MURPHY
We're missing a few, you know.

GRATTAN
Our seductive Volonty walked into it, and the rest of our people are in the clink for breaking the blue laws. Or so they said. God, Sunday around here! Hell's the only place open. Really for feely the sheriff. Or not feely the sheriff.

HOUDINI
This Volonty?

GRATTAN

Our seductive Volonty—dancer, acrobat, high-wire artist. Anything that moves like a woman.

BILL

They ain't met us yet.

GRATTAN

(To BILL.*)*
Get Murphy off the bottle. Oh, well, no show tonight.
(In full voice.)
This is Bill, our Man of Steel; Mrs. Murphy, the Juggler, you should see her five guns; this is Ariana, the Spanish Fly; the clowns, Whitsun and Epictetus, they double as dwarfs and they're the angels in the Living Statues. And little Henry Thoreau, Mrs. Murphy's kid. He's inside the automaton, writing and drawing. There's your formal hello. How many handcuffs can you get out of in ten minutes?

BEATRICE

He can get out of any lock.

HOUDINI

You took me on as an expert, didn't you? What have you got around here?

BILL

He's got a strongbox.

MRS. MURPHY

Nothing in it.

GRATTAN
Leave the box out.
(HOUDINI *goes to the trunk and kicks it.*)

HOUDINI
Yes. Made in Boston. Reinforced, inside and out. Lock me in.
(*He gets in and pulls the lid down. They fasten the hasps
down, and then the big lock.* BEATRICE *flings her shawl over
the top of the trunk.*)

BILL
He can't get out of that.

BEATRICE
Can't he?

GRATTAN
We could use a man who could get out of anything.

HOUDINI
That's me.
(HOUDINI *is out.*)

GRATTAN
Bill, give him back his watch.
(BILL, *who has lifted it, returns it; he hates to do it.*)

BILL
Anyone can do that.
(BILL *climbs in.*)

GRATTAN
Look, Houdini, let's go for a walk.

BEATRICE

In this rain?

GRATTAN

First things first. If you can do a lock like that—you know, that's a rickety hoosegow down there. It looks solid, but I have an idea—

HOUDINI

I just do that for show, Mr. Grattan.

GRATTAN

The way you got out of that trunk! Look, boy, I saw you at Tony Pastor's, in the noise and the smoke. A lot of green kids, amateurs, trying their stuff. Young hopefuls, nothing much. Then this youngster, full of fire, full of sex, yourself. Full of pride, full of muscle—fireworks over a city asleep. Breaking your lungs to get out of those chains, and everybody could see. But what did you have in those places? Bottom billing, if anything. Why don't you ask where the animals are?

HOUDINI

All right, where are they?

GRATTAN

Fool! We don't have any. But we could. We could light out of here, and go straight up. And that's what will happen if you do what's needed, boy. You'll be up there, everybody will know what you are. But if you're fool enough to say no, the whole deal is off, because of the spot I'm in. Jake didn't show up with his little black bag full of spinach; they're in the clink, and we're through—half our people! And no billing for you, no "Modern Master of Mystery."

HOUDINI
Yes.

BEATRICE
I'll get my coat.

HOUDINI
She's an asset.

GRATTAN
Absolutely no. Not possible.

HOUDINI
Bess, you stay here. I'll be back.

BEATRICE
Harry, please. All right. Safe home.

HOUDINI
What is the exact time?

BEATRICE
6:15 P.M.

GRATTAN
Coming, Houdini?
(They go out.)

HOUDINI
Which way to the clink?

MRS. MURPHY
(*Sounds from inside the trunk.*)
Never mind.

BEATRICE
He can't get out.
(*To* MRS. MURPHY.)
It makes me feel shut in myself.

MRS. MURPHY
Yes, honey, me too.

EPICTETUS
What kind of songs do you sing?

BEATRICE
Anything.

MRS. MURPHY
Hear that? Like her man: anything.

BEATRICE
I think he expects to do tricks — streamers, hoops — he's working on inventions.

WHITSUN
Inventions! He better do what Grattan tells him.

MRS. MURPHY
Or you'll find a way, hey, Whitsun?

WHITSUN

Well, we're . . . persuasive. He wouldn't like an accident to his hands, would he?

EPICTETUS

Never mind about *him.* What about you?

BEATRICE

I'm his assistant.

WHITSUN

And more also. We'll teach you to be at the tent flap while the crowd is coming in. Sometimes there's quite a bit of cash —

BEATRICE

Ah, no.

MRS. MURPHY

Nothing too risky, child.

(To CLOWNS.*)*

Ah, take it up with the magic man himself — if he ever gets back.

BEATRICE

(To MRS. MURPHY.*)*

I'll do whatever it takes to help Harry.

WHITSUN

Can you, even when they're yelling?

Can you, to get them ready for Volonty, on her high wire?

Can you, when we're nipping most of your clothes off?

BEATRICE

Try me.

MRS. MURPHY

Try her. You could be a clown too—

BEATRICE

Not yet . . . I don't think he can get out of there.

EPICTETUS

Oh, he's all right. Get the paint box.

MRS. MURPHY

She's worried about her husband. Let her alone.

BEATRICE

Come on. My face.

MRS. MURPHY

Get the key, Whitsun!
(BILL *is out. Exit* WHITSUN, EPICTETUS, *and* BILL.)
They have the songbook privilege for this circus, and we could cut you in on that. They sing like a rusty door. There should be a few cents in there somewhere for you.
(PUD *enters with paint box.*)
Here, I'll do it. And you get her clothes. Your husband's crazy about you—and his work—isn't he?

BEATRICE

He takes delight in what he does. His skills. He likes being loaded down and confined. He likes even more to break out. He loves to be watched.

MRS. MURPHY
You've been married less than a year—?

BEATRICE
Yes.

MRS. MURPHY
Your mother pleased about it?

BEATRICE
She hasn't spoken to me since.

MRS. MURPHY
Fainted on the spot, didn't she?

BEATRICE
She thinks I married a jail breaker.

MRS. MURPHY
I guess he learned his stuff while he was doing time.

BEATRICE
No, he never. What does Volonty really do, Mrs. Murphy?

MRS. MURPHY
Volonty dances on air. Up there—she stands on it, feels it, pulls secrets out of it, sends her body through it . . . Sometimes I hate her.
(*Laughs.*)
Air's her element.
(WHITSUN *and* EPICTETUS *return.*)

41

EPICTETUS

A most adequate introduction, to these associations that bode well. And your fee, in excess of your salary, will be two dollars for fourteen shows. How do you like it?

BEATRICE

I like it very much!

WHITSUN

When we get our pay.

EPICTETUS

Ah, no, honey, you'll get yours.

BEATRICE

If you don't mind my asking—how do you manage that?

EPICTETUS

Well, now, honey, I wouldn't ask too many questions. That's Volonty's territory.

MRS. MURPHY

She has a right!

EPICTETUS

We pass through the audience. We're selling ice cream, right? And song sheets, right? Well, they've got pockets—? Lovely and deep.

WHITSUN

If we weren't here, we'd be off at the wars, picking a pocket.

WHITSUN and EPICTETUS
(Speaking, changing tone.)
Wars are for dead men,
Wars are for jerks,
I want a woman—
(BEATRICE stands up. She wears a pointed yoke of lace and tights. Her painted face is very moving.)
Like fireworks!
(VOLONTY bursts through the tiger's mouth. HOUDINI, GRATTAN, and the FAT GIRL follow.)

VOLONTY
Out of that place! My wonders! Bring me my robe. You're Bess.

BEATRICE
You're Volonty.

VOLONTY
(To HOUDINI.)
My liberator!

GRATTAN
Pack everything. We're clearing out. He picked those locks like chestnuts.

HOUDINI
It was a pleasure . . . What is the time?

BEATRICE
(Looks for her watch; gets it back from one of the CLOWNS. The situation is a little different; she slaps him lightly.)
It's exactly 6:55 P.M.

43

FAT GIRL
    Free at 6:55 post meridian.

GRATTAN
    Give them some whiskey and some chow that's really hot.
    Some speed, there.

BEATRICE
    (To HOUDINI, *of her costume.)*
    Like it?

HOUDINI
    We'll keep it.

GRATTAN
    He picked those locks like chestnuts.

BILL
    Come on. We don't swallow that.

VOLONTY
    Sure, he dissolved the jail.

WHITSUN
    Lock man! He's a master pickpocket.

FAT GIRL
    We were locked in. He got us out.

HOUDINI
    There are chains. There is freedom. There are keys.

VOLONTY

Is there anything besides opening locks that fascinates you, Mr. Houdini?

HOUDINI

The details of a lock interest me. The sliding bow or shackle, the bolts of the older kind of lock; the padlock, the kind that hangs on something; the ones with tumblers . . .

VOLONTY

We're tumblers . . .

HOUDINI

We're keys, we open them. The ancient locks found in Nineveh made of wood, the ones on chastity belts, the Yale lock that has a tongue on its back which projects into the lock itself, the latest protector locks that must have a little play; and the movement called tentative; duplex locks of three kinds: palace motion, easy action, and Scotch spring. Do you know there are locks that will open at a whisper? The whisper is the key. Do you know about the sleep of locks? Like us they rest; sometimes they have to be jarred awake, kicked awake, jiggled, and they start working again. They have bodies; and I think they love and hate.

VOLONTY

What kinds of words do you have for your own body?

HOUDINI

Who has words for such things? What's this called beside an armpit? What's this beside the inside of the elbow? What's this, the back of the knee? Some medical student told me "post-patellar" . . . That can't be right, can it?

VOLONTY

You mean the vulnerable places? Female places, I think they are.

HOUDINI

All are vulnerable, male or female. My body is my instrument of work. I work to know it, to make it stronger, more sensitive, more vulnerable, more aware . . .

GRATTAN

All this stuff about lox! Wait till he discovers bagels! Why don't you ask what else you do?

HOUDINI

I read it from the face of my wife.

GRATTAN

What you do, boy!
(He is drinking through this.)
Suppose you could open that strongbox?

HOUDINI

Not interested.

GRATTAN

Have one?

HOUDINI

(He never drinks.)
Thank you, not just now.

GRATTAN

I knew you the first moment at Tony Pastor's. In the slop and the old smoke. Among the green and halfway kids. And then a youngster like yourself, full of pride, full of muscle, full of sex, full of skill. Breaking your lungs, you were, and letting us see. Well?

HOUDINI

I'm to be a clown, as well as a magician and a lock expert?

GRATTAN

Sure, and everything else. Drum-thumper, acrobat, mind-reader, clairvoyant—

HOUDINI

I'm no good at talking.

GRATTAN

They'll swallow anything. You know what else they want? Sometimes they howl for a wild man. He eats raw meat and cigars, he chews the heads off chickens. Can you roar? Sure you can roar. You're Borneo if you're staying?
(He sees a flicker.)

HOUDINI

(Makes up his mind.)
I'm staying if you take my manager, Marco Bone.
(Inflated; he has no manager. GRATTAN *holds his head; one more!)*
He runs a shooting gallery.

GRATTAN

Every place needs a shooting gallery!

BEATRICE
First week's salary in advance.

VOLONTY
Dimes! We've got zero.

GRATTAN
We've got Houdini.
(HOUDINI *is already in the trunk. It opens out into an entire world, starlit, lit red and dark, the red and gold of the circus turned into something even further, a reach of space.* HOUDINI's *movements in the trunk carry a grave sureness that there is a way out. A kind of tunnel. He touches the ideas of the lock. All the parts of his body are touched by these. As* HOUDINI *rises from the trunk, he reaches down behind him and pulls* MARCO BONE *up with him and out.*)

MARCO BONE
Of course, I'm with you, but only out of season. When Coney Island opens, back to the shooting gallery.
(*Sees* VOLONTY.)
Don't tell me. It begins with a "V."

VOLONTY
Everybody's mind-readers around here. We should be rich.

VOLONTY (*Song: "Beer and Bacon"*)
WHEN YOU SEE A WOMAN RIDING THE AIR
WELL, YOU SEE A WOMAN PLAYING WITH FIRE,
A WOMAN MADE OF STORM AND DESIRE
AND SHE LOVES THE WHOLE DAMN ZOO.
BUT YOU CAN BE SURE, WHATEVER I DO,
THAT I NEED MY BEER AND BACON TOO.

I WAKE EVERY NIGHT AT 4 A.M.
AND I TELL MY DREAMS TO THE MAN WHO IS THERE,
DREAMS OF ANIMALS NOT LIKE HIM —
A WOMAN WHO RIDES ON FIRE AND AIR
LOVES TO DREAM WITH THE WHOLE DAMN ZOO
BUT I NEED MY BEER AND BACON TOO.

MY DREAMS RIDE OUT FROM THE HIGHEST WIRE
BODIES LIKE BUBBLES OF COLOR DOWN THERE,
THE FEEL OF PEOPLE OF FLESH AND FIRE
STREAMING TOWARD ME ALONG THE AIR —
BUT I MAKE IT CLEAR, WHATEVER I DO,
THAT I NEED MY BEER AND BACON TOO.

(Shift of scene. HOUDINI *and* BEATRICE *in their room — really their circus truck — really deep into their privacy.)*

BEATRICE

Can you really chop a woman to bits?

HOUDINI

I could kiss you to bits. No more bottom billing, after a dog act. We'll do it all. You walked out of your house.

BEATRICE

You ran away when you were twelve.

HOUDINI

I went back. You never did.

BEATRICE

I saw something so powerful on the beach that day.

49

HOUDINI

I can stream flame from my fingers and toes and sex and every inch of me. I begin to speak. I say something that makes everyone stand up and cry out—

BEATRICE

You do something to make me cry out. What do you say?

HOUDINI

I don't know. Or I won't talk. Or I don't want to talk.
(Shift of scene. VOLONTY *and* MARCO BONE.*)*

VOLONTY

Then you travel. Back to Coney Island.

MARCO BONE

Not just now. Now I set up the targets.

VOLONTY

And the sheriff?

MARCO BONE

(As an announcer.)
No, the sheriffs never catch up with us. In a thousand tank towns. The Houdinis show what they can do. They read minds and they tell customers the sex of their children born and unborn. The Houdinis send shivers up the spines of thousands. He chops her up, he sends her up a rope standing in the air . . . the old Indian Rope Trick. She fights for her song—a lovely woman fighting for a song—and the extra two dollars every week. He pitches the tent like anybody. It all adds up.

HOUDINI, BEATRICE, VOLONTY, and MARCO BONE
  (Song: "Nickels and Dimes")
>   HARD TIMES, TERRIBLE TIMES,
>   WE'RE DOWN TO NICKLES AND DIMES—
>   MAYBE YOU'RE . . . SONS AND DAUGHTERS
>   WILL GET THEIR HANDS . . . DOLLARS AND
>   QUARTERS . . .
>   MAYBE OIL . . . DIAMONDS AND STEEL,
>   MAYBE AN AIRPLANE OR AN AUTOMOBILE
>   BUT NOW ALL WE'VE GOT IS THE STEERING WHEEL—
>   BUT JUST NOW . . . ALL THAT'S REAL
>   IS WHAT WE FEEL
>   AND THAT AIN'T STEEL,
>   NOT OIL,
>   NOT DIAMONDS—
>   HARD TIMES, TERRIBLE TIMES
>   WE'RE DOWN TO NICKLES AND DIMES—

HOUDINI

Sure, I do séances. People want to believe that. You lead their eyes, you pull a string. You lead the bull.
(He's a torero.)
They *want* it. The minute I can, no more séances. I'm convinced there's more money to be made, once they see who I am.

VOLONTY

A real escape artist. Tell your fortune, good looking?

HOUDINI

No, thanks. Against my religion.

VOLONTY

What religion would that be?

HOUDINI

What I live by. Pompous as ever. And, of course, born Jewish. My father said we're not magicians because of what Moses did.

VOLONTY

Kill the Egyptian?

HOUDINI

There's that, but you know when they were in the desert? No water, but there was the cloud by day. And God told Moses to strike the rock with his staff. Water gushed forth. Moses let them believe it was all his doing; he didn't give credit. That's why he wasn't allowed to go into the Promised Land. And we're not to *be magicians.*

VOLONTY

And whose credit? Oh, I see. But you're a magician.

HOUDINI

Come on. You know better. I'm an illusionist.

VOLONTY

Same difference.

HOUDINI

Want your fortune told?
(*Enter* BEATRICE, *with a huge flat basket. She is dressed in lace yoke and tights.*)

VOLONTY

Some people will do anything.
(*Exit* HOUDINI. *To* BEATRICE.)
Tell your fortune, young lady?

BEATRICE

Not by feeling, Volonty.

VOLONTY

Your fortune's all over you, Bess . . . devoted and not devoted,
hot and cold, afraid and not afraid, giving, withholding, set
on having your life, like him—and loving, loving, loving,
come hell or high water.

BEATRICE

That's not my fortune, that's what I started out with.

VOLONTY

That's the foundation.
(*Enter* HOUDINI *with a coiled rope and a sword.*)

HOUDINI

All right, set it up: The Disappearing Woman!
(*The basket in the middle of the stage, with the rope coiled
flat in the bottom.* BEATRICE *gets into the basket, curled; she
raises her back once to show the audience she is there. Then*
HOUDINI *puts the lid on the basket, calls "All right?" and be-
gins to thrust the sword into the basket, at one place after the
other.* BEATRICE *pushes the lid off, shows him that all is well,
and subsides again.* VOLONTY *watches.* HOUDINI *makes thrust
after thrust with the sword.*

53

The MAGIC: *if this is done by verbal means, the pillar of smoke stands in stage center.)*

HOUDINI

Standing on air, the cloud by day,
A woman climbing the cloud.
Sex and the cloud, a climbing woman.
She begins to dissolve.
The woman in pieces.
Slowly, they rise up woman again,
The woman turns into air.
(HOUDINI *has disappeared.* BEATRICE *takes the rope and sword and exits.* VOLONTY *announces.)*

VOLONTY

And now, ladies and gentlemen, what you have all been howling for! The man who comes out of the jungle, as he is, in the flesh, untamed, untrained. He's got a language all his own! So, ladies, watch out you don't get pulled apart, limb from limb! Here he is, your wild man: Borneo!

HOUDINI, ENSEMBLE, VOLONTY, and BEATRICE
(*Dance: Borneo*)

(HOUDINI *leaps out on a high stage, naked except for fur colors. The* WOMEN OF THE ENSEMBLE *scatter before him in excitement and mock fear, yelping, growling, barking. The men shake their banners; they identify with the women and with* BORNEO *by turns, but it goes to* BORNEO *in a stamping excitement.*

The WOMEN *are on their backs, in rows, legs waving before* BORNEO. VOLONTY *in the foreground, delighted, pretend-*

ing fear. It is delightful and "primitive" and rules out any-
thing that is not exclusively physical. At the height, VOLONTY
calls out "One more time!" The beat comes to its strongest.

At the end of Borneo, BEATRICE *is thrust through his legs, be-*
neath him, in place of VOLONTY. *Exit* ENSEMBLE. *They are*
in their wagon.)

BEATRICE
(*Cries out.*)
Harry!
(*She is wearing tights and a luminous necklace.*)

HOUDINI
Did I terrify you, Bess?

BEATRICE
Borneo took over.

HOUDINI
Only for a moment. Borneo knows, you know. I want to get
out of this circus.

BEATRICE
I love your wildness.

HOUDINI
What I use is control. But no more going around cemeteries
for the information for mind-reading acts.

BEATRICE
You know you love that.

ENSEMBLE *(As* CECILIA*)*
The graveyard is a trap, Ehrich.

HOUDINI
Borneo's a trap. I want them to look at *me.* I want to do something they'll believe. The only real things I've done are make myself stronger, have you, and get Volonty out of jail.

BEATRICE
I see a man in pieces, his beautiful strong legs and trunk and arms all severed and on the ground.

HOUDINI
That's you. It's the Indian Rope Trick.

BEATRICE
Slowly, the man in pieces begins to come together. A great golden snake is wound around his arms and legs and he stands up. I adore him.

ENSEMBLE *(As* CECILIA*)*
Those iron bars fall away.

HOUDINI
Maybe something about a jail. You're right, Bess. The pieces are joining. I want to talk to mother. I want to work out something with Marco Bone.
(MARCO BONE *appears.*)

MARCO BONE
All you have to do is break out of the strongest jail there is.

HOUDINI

Marco! It's fall in Coney Island.
(*They hug.*)

MARCO BONE

They're nailing up the Tunnel of Love for winter. You should
have your own show.

HOUDINI

No more Borneos.

MARCO BONE

Yes, Bess, a new dress. Prettier than ever. Here is what I pro-
pose. The strongest jail—I'll get the word on it; some money
will bring the reporters and a couple of photographers. I'll have
them ready for you. They'll strip you—Harry!

HOUDINI

Just so the pictures are made.

MARCO BONE

They'll strip and search you. They lock you up—your clothes
in one cell, you in another. And then—
(*Switch.*)

HOUDINI

They take pictures.

BEATRICE

They'll search you for a key.

MARCO BONE

Thoroughly.

ACT ONE, SCENE THREE

(The city jail, the WARDEN'*s office before us, at the side; the prisoners in their cells, seen as* HOUDINI *sees them; in a place of great excitement, a place he can break out of. The colors are brilliant, green baize for the* WARDEN'*s office; the locks are glass brick, like water, the colors fluoresce. The bars are black. Even the door of the* WARDEN'*s office is treated in this way. All keys are Lucite. They glow.*

BEATRICE *is with the* WARDEN. *She is very flirtatious, jaunty in a way we have not seen, aggressive. The* WARDEN *is a great beefsteak of a man, sure of his vigor and authority, with no nerves at all.)*

WARDEN
(Laughing.)
And what did you do?

BEATRICE
Well, I said something very rude.

WARDEN

Fool he was, to stop at all. When we step out, the evening won't end like that? Tonight?
(He comes around the desk, takes BEATRICE *in his arms. Knock on the door.* TURNKEY *puts his head in.)*

TURNKEY

He's still snooping around, boss.

WARDEN

(Standing back, official again.)
Bring him in then.

BEATRICE

Have a heart. We're doing a story about you, Warden.

WARDEN

Mr. Hooten has plenty to go on. With your notes, honey.
(Enter HOUDINI *and the* DOCTORS. *They strip him and begin to examine.)*

MARCO BONE

(Entering.)
Here we are, "Murderer's Row."

ENSEMBLE

(A body count.)
One, two, three, four . . .

WARDEN

All right, Hooten.

HOUDINI
  What is the exact time?
  (*Meaningful "out" look to* BEATRICE, *slight humorous resent-*
  ment of WARDEN.)

MARCO BONE
  What is the exact time?

ENSEMBLE
  What is the exact time?
  What is the exact time?
  What is the exact time?

BEATRICE
  6:48 P.M.

ENSEMBLE
  6:48 P.M.
  6:48 P.M.
  6:48 P.M.
  (*Exit* BEATRICE.)

MARCO BONE
  Examine him, gentlemen, as only a physician can . . .
  (*The physical examination.*)

PHYSICIANS
  Mouth, Nose, Anus, Eyes,
  Toenails, Fingernails, Ears,
  Mouth, Nose, Anus, Eyes . . .

FIRST PHYSICIAN
  Any scars?

PHYSICIANS
No scars. No fresh wounds.

FIRST PHYSICIAN
He's a fool. How can he think those doors would open?
But . . .
(Grudgingly.)
. . . he's got the finest physique I ever saw.

WARDEN
So long, Hooten. See you in the morning.
(HOUDINI *is passed into a cell.*)

PRISONER
Where are your clothes?

HOUDINI
I hocked them. What are you in for?

PRISONER
What are you in for?

HOUDINI
I want to open this lock.

PRISONER
Me too. Nobody opens Jo Guitar's place.

HOUDINI
Who's Jo Guitar?

PRISONER
This is his cell. He killed the President.

HOUDINI
   You killed Garfield?
   (He is working fast.)

PRISONER
   Jo Guitar did. I put a pillow over your wife.

HOUDINI
   Now!
   (He opens the door.)
   Come out!
   (Brings the man out. He goes to the next cell. Points.)
   What's he?

PRISONER
   Child-knifer.

HOUDINI
   (Points along the cells.)
   And him? And him?

PRISONER
   Cop-killer. Mass-rapist. Nothing much.
   (HOUDINI opens two of the doors forcibly, sexually, the third lock with a whisper, he wakes the fourth. He moves the PRIS-ONERS, each into another cell. They react in their own ways. Fighting among the PRISONERS.)

SECOND PRISONER
   What the hell you doing, man? Me in his cell? No!

THIRD PRISONER
   And now the next lock!

FOURTH PRISONER
Can you get me out of here?

HOUDINI
(Looking at him in despair.)
No.

PRISONER
Warden . . . get this man out!

HOUDINI
Warden . . . Warden!
(To WARDEN, *who is in the jail almost as much as the others.*)
What are you in for?

WARDEN
(Realizing the change.)
Can't be done! You're made, young fellow. By God! I'll get these locks changed. We'll get new ones invented! This'll never be done again! Houdini! That's a name I'll remember. You're the greatest of them all! And your wife? Where's she gone?
(HOUDINI *does not answer.*)

HOUDINI
(To PRISONERS, *with intensity.*)
Forgive me.

MARCO BONE
He did it! He's made.

HOUDINI
(In the outer jail.)
What was the time?

MARCO BONE
Three minutes, ten seconds.

ENSEMBLE
He did it! He's made.

HOUDINI
Got any ice cream?

MARCO BONE
Get the man some ice cream.

ENSEMBLE
He did it! He's made! Get the man some ice cream.

HOUDINI
It was better than I hoped! Marco, you're my personal manager. You'll start at . . . I don't know . . .

MARCO BONE
When the papers hit the street, you're as good as rich.

HOUDINI
Can the shooting gallery wait?

MARCO BONE
In the hope of the resurrection.

HOUDINI
> And the strong lady, your true love?

MARCO BONE
> I might have a new true love.

WARDEN
> You're made.

HOUDINI
> Who was the man in solitary?

WARDEN
> You wouldn't care to know him.

HOUDINI
> What did he do?

WARDEN
> You answer one question.

REPORTER
> How did you do it?

HOUDINI
> I swam through. Come on, boys, I'll see you at the house.

WARDEN
> Now they'll be saying, "Houdini, get me out."

HOUDINI
> I can't even get you out.

WARDEN
  Where's Mrs. Houdini?

BLACK PRISONER and PRISONERS   *(Song: "Hostility")*

BLACK PRISONER
        THE MAN WHO OPENED MY PRISON DOOR
        HAS PUT ME BACK IN JAIL.
        NO CHANCE TO PLEAD MY INNOCENCE,
        OR GET OUT OF HERE ON BAIL.
        SOMEONE SHOWED ME FREE,
        AND DROVE ME DEEPER IN MY MISERY.

PRISONERS
        OH, HOSTILITY,
        HOSTILITY.

BLACK PRISONER
        THE MAN WHO SHOWED ME MY FREEDOM,
        A MAN WHO NEVER DID TIME,
        HE MADE IT A SHELL GAME, FREEDOM,
        SHUFFLING CRIME AND CRIME.
        SOMEONE SHOWED ME FREE
        HE SWITCHED MY PUNISHMENT AND MISERY . . .

PRISONERS
        OH, HOSTILITY,
        HOSTILITY.

(The scene transforms: HOUDINI'*s home.* REPORTERS *come in, as do* HOUDINI, MARCO BONE, BEATRICE, VOLONTY.*)*

ENSEMBLE
(They are reporters in the doorway. And children.)
—Sure, he had something hidden!
—But the doctors said he was clean.
—Those locks were fixed for you, come on.
—One more picture.
(The children.)
—Find some money in my ear.
—Disappear me, Houdini!

BEATRICE
I thought your mother would object to nakedness.

ENSEMBLE *(In CECILIA's voice.)*
Would you expect the children in the fiery furnace to keep their clothes on?

HOUDINI
I need something else.

BEATRICE
There you were—opening the doors—

ENSEMBLE *(In CECILIA's voice.)*
He needs to throw himself against all things.

BEATRICE
You walked right out of that jail.

HOUDINI
A way *through.*

ENSEMBLE *(In* CECILIA's *voice.)*
A way through.

HOUDINI
I'll just go out and see those children.
(Exits.)

VOLONTY
Sounds like an escape to me. All that foofarrah about an escape hatch.

MARCO BONE
Greatest thing since the oubliette.

BEATRICE
It's really a tunnel he's talking about. You're not closed in, everything has a passage. If you work with the forces.

VOLONTY
What about the mystery of the sealed room? Or the bird in the egg?

BEATRICE
The chick feeds on the walls of his room, and at the last moment, he is strong enough. His prison cell is only a shell.

MARCO BONE
But the chick has grown a tooth to peck with. A pecker. What do you see, Volonty?

VOLONTY
I see my prophet man, announcing the magician.

MARCO BONE

    Am I your man?

    (She does not answer.)

    Well, Beatrice . . . He's beginning to talk to them. That's your doing.

    (They shake hands.)

BEATRICE

    I always wanted to be your friend.

MARCO BONE

    Not when you turned up, wearing the dress his mother made for you. You gave me a dragon look when you thought I didn't see.

BEATRICE

    I didn't know what you'd want of him.

MARCO BONE

    And now?

BEATRICE

    Now, I know you help him, and start him, and are always there for him.

MARCO BONE

    Like you, in a way.

BEATRICE

    You're the star in heaven with his red companion.

MARCO BONE

    He's the star in heaven with his red companion.

BEATRICE
> Close, Marco.
> *(She goes to* HOUDINI.*)*

MARCO BONE
> Have you heard how the basket was woven about him in Holland? Have you heard how he was sealed in a paper bag and left it intact . . . which is more than the way most things are left? Have you heard how he collected signed affidavits of escapes from every jail he visited and has written proof of his ability to free himself from every lock and bond that any challenger could create?

VOLONTY
> What are you, a kind of double for Houdini?

MARCO BONE
> Sure, we're the same. Sure, we're different.

VOLONTY
> Do you love him?

MARCO BONE
> Is there a way not to love Houdini? Sure I love him. And I have ideas, big ideas for him. I'm going to make him famous.

VOLONTY
> Why don't you make something for yourself?

MARCO BONE
> Yes . . . yes.

VOLONTY

 I see a man coming towards me . . .

MARCO BONE

 Yes, men do go forward, getting things, out of their women, into their women, for them, against them.

VOLONTY

 There's something in the air between us, right here. Above the ground. I could tell your fortune.

MARCO BONE

 Go ahead.

VOLONTY

 Here, this arm . . . you contradict yourself, you'll go far and you'll return. Your neck. Your neck! Some people might say they're depraved, but you really mean it! Your shoulders. You want your body to find everything you can't find . . . and something sly, something loyal, something plain with all that fancy.

MARCO BONE

 Tell me more.

VOLONTY

 Have you heard how he gave 300 pairs of shoes to all the poor boys of a town in Scotland? And broke all the box-office records too? And then there was a new dress . . .

MARCO BONE

 Yes, a new dress.

VOLONTY

Queen Victoria died before she could wear a certain new dress. It went on sale for 150 pounds in a dressmaker's window.

MARCO BONE

Houdini spied it and bought it.

VOLONTY

He sent for his mother and took over the palm garden of the best hotel in Budapest, the city she left weeping in her young disgrace. He crowned his mother queen in that dress and poured a thousand gold dollars into her lap.

MARCO BONE

The jackpot!

VOLONTY

So what if he borrowed carfare to leave town? Why remember that?
(*Enter* HOUDINI.)

MARCO BONE

I remember everything, don't I, Harry?

HOUDINI

That's how he knows everything. Why, what did she say?

MARCO BONE

Your mother? It's not what she says. She has a quality of . . . I don't know, it's really ecstasy. And the delicious stuffed stuff! A target for my gallery.

VOLONTY

And what does Marco know?

MARCO BONE

Oh, we know, we know. Something about what you can do, Volonty, something about what you need, hey?

VOLONTY

I? Who have everything? Safe above you on the high wire?

HOUDINI

We won't give it away, ever, Volonty.

VOLONTY

Give it away!

HOUDINI

There has to be a lot more to it than that, in the sky where you are, and down here too.
(HOUDINI *walks to the pillows.* HOUDINI *and* BESS *in bed.* BESS, *waiting for him, does not speak.*)
You knew, that first day, what the magic was, between us. Between the people on the beach: the fat man, the chorus girls, the sailor. You knew what I could speak to: fear, and every muscle in people's bodies. I have to go further, Bess. A risk of life.

ACT ONE, SCENE FOUR

(River Music begins. Ice, river. Music down for the following.)

MARCO BONE

It is an icy day in the middle of winter, with the wind blowing off the frozen river. My axe is all right and I've got plenty of rope. Six inches of it will be worth a dollar to the onlookers.

The doctors asked him not to. And the theater people. There is plenty of money at stake. The river is sealed up, thick, like a bank vault. "What of it?" said Houdini. "Can't you cut through ice?"
(The stage is the frozen river; MARCO BONE's axe handle slips as he stamps it on the ice. Reporters and opponents with chains gather around HOUDINI.)

OPPONENTS

—Ah, he's got a diving bell waiting for him, down there!
—A log fire.
—Somebody go and check!

MARCO BONE

Why not? Anybody?

(Silence.)

Too cold for you? What is it, this ice? It's water. And it isn't.

It's colorless. And it's crystal. And reliable—forms at
     freezing every time. Hey?

You're a river. Yes, you.

You pour a river down your throat every day, all your life.

Ice? It's water that floats on water.

It locks. It grows, tight.

It's on top.

The river is underneath, flowing fast.

We cut a hole in the ice—

(They hack and saw the ice.)

There are currents, pulling.

There's fish, and slime, and seaweed in long scarves, in
     chains, and the eels!

What are you afraid of?

You're not down there!

Cold, super-cool, solid, the weight of houses, the weight of
     towers pressing down on you.

Who's going down there? Houdini, that's who!

HOUDINI

(Chains. Music up.)

Load them on me!

(Cries out in a supernaturally loud voice.)

Amara Elon!

HOUDINI   *(Song: "Chains, Freedom, Keys")*
          THERE ARE CHAINS—
          THERE IS FREEDOM—

THERE ARE KEYS —
    AND OF THESE, CHAINS ARE STRONG
FREEDOM'S ENDLESS, KEYS ARE GREAT
AND WE
ARE THE GREATEST OF THESE,
THE GREATEST
OF THESE.

THERE ARE CHAINS —
THERE IS FREEDOM —
THERE ARE KEYS —
    AND OF THESE,
THERE ARE THOSE I HAVE SEEN
I HAVE HEARD
AND I KNOW
I HAVE SEEN
I HAVE HEARD
AND I KNOW —
THERE ARE CHAINS —
THERE IS FREEDOM —
THERE ARE KEYS —
AND THE GREATEST OF THESE
CAN FREE THE WORLD.

MARCO BONE
    You're telling them something they want to hear.

HOUDINI
    I'm just doing it.

MARCO BONE
    You're saying it. With yourself!

(They chop a hole in the ice. HOUDINI *lowers himself through it; that is, the great plastic sheet is raised above him to the height of the stage, which now becomes the river. As he sinks, he struggles with the chains, casts them off on the floor of the cold river. The sheet swings forward to face the audience.* HOUDINI *makes for the hole in the ice, now between the audience and himself.)*

REPORTERS and OPPONENTS

— Guard the riverbanks, he's faking it!

— He's got a rope around him, they'll pull him out downstream!

— Nobody can live in water that cold, not more than a few minutes.

— He's got a car waiting for him somewhere — set up search lights!

— No. No. No. No. He's really under there.

HOUDINI and ENSEMBLE *(Song: "In the Dark, in the Deep Dark")*

DOWN DOWN SILVER GREEN

DOWN DOWN SILVER BROWN

SILVER BROWN

SILVER GREEN

                    NOW THE TEETH

SILVER LOW

                    NOW THE GOLD

SILVER BLUE

SILVER LOW

                    NOW THE DREAD

SILVER

                    NOW THE BEASTS

SILVER BLUE

SILVER

                    NOW THE TEETH

DOWN DOWN SILVER BLACK
                              DOOR TO THE AIR
                     BLACK
                              NO DOOR!
                     BLACK

                     THE ROPE!
                     TRY THE ROPE!
                     THE AXE!
                     NOW!
                     CHAINS OF WATER.
                     DREAD.
                     BREATH.
                     NO TIME.

                     NO I'M . . .
               FIGHT FREE
               UP AIR
               ICE BLACK (ICE BLACK)
FIGHT FREE   I'LL HACK THIS RIVER OPEN!
FIGHT FREE   TOO LATE.
UP AIR   TOO LATE.
FIGHT FREE   EXTREE
UP AIR   EXTREE
ICE BLACK (ICE BLACK)   READ ALL
FIGHT FREE   ABOUT IT
FIGHT FREE   HOUDINI DIES
UP AIR   IN THE ICE
ICE BLACK (ICE BLACK)   HOUDINI DIES
FIGHT FREE   IN THE ICE
          HOUDINI DIES IN THE ICE
          HOUDINI DIES IN THE ICE
          HOUDINI DIES IN THE ICE

(Doors of ice. Doors of ice. Doors of wood. A colored door. A pale door. An ivory door. BEATRICE *appearing as the doors pass. She hears the death of* HOUDINI *cried by the newsboys.* HOUDINI *stands there, gasping, naked, trailing a branch of seaweed.)*

HOUDINI
I had to.
Get through.
To you.
*(*BEATRICE *rushes to the embrace. The telephone rings.* HOUDINI *breaks out, goes to the phone and picks it up. Into the phone.)*
Hello, mother.
Yes.
I'm fine.
(Pink streamers of light.)

CECILIA'S VOICE
Oh, I'm home.
Holding the fort.
But I'm with you.
Wherever you are.
(He hangs up and comes back to her. She stands frozen, hands over her breasts. Afflicted physically by this. The words overtake her.)

BEATRICE
What are you trying to do — God Jesus! Killing everything —
And the goddamn fucking sun, what about the sunlight?
(Changing tone.)
And me and me? What about —

Put yourself in the goddamn crawling rivercunt—
They yell you dead—your riverwife rivermother—
and you bloody Jesus know you can make anything—
life—or breakthrough—you blazing man you always
were, but you make fucking sin suicide—that's a deep . . .
Why do you do it to me? And I pay rivers!
(He tries to enter the telephone wire.)
What makes you think you could find any hole?
Anywhere?
(She really sees him now.)
Dripping life life-fucking but you deny, Christ,
it's a blazing man do anything—
(She breaks and goes to him.)
only blaze and somehow—

INTERMISSION

ACT TWO

ACT TWO, SCENE ONE

ACT TWO follows directly from ACT ONE *with no passage of time, except, of course, for the audience.*

*(*BEATRICE *kisses, warms, dresses* HOUDINI. *Black pants, incredibly white shirt, no tie, red suspenders. He is very still during this, being brought back to full life as it goes on.)*

ENSEMBLE   *(Song: "The Mediums")*
(Surrounding them both.)
   I SEE A TREE HALF GREEN HALF BURNING —
   I SEE A MAN. I CANNOT SEE HIS EYES —
   I SEE A WOMAN PUTTING ON A RING —
   I SEE A GOLD KEY. I SEE A GOLD KEY —
   I SEE FIRE. I SEE FIRE. IT IS HELL —
   OR IS IT THE FOUNDATION OF SOMETHING?

HOUDINI
(Standing clear of BEATRICE.*)*
My mind is open. I have always wanted to believe.
(He puts his arms out, as if to touch.)
. . . But I have seen nothing, heard nothing that makes me think they can talk to us. We talk to them —

MARCO BONE
    We talk to the living?

HOUDINI
    Further. We talk to the dead, but—

MARCO BONE
    (Does not want HOUDINI *to talk like this.)*
    This is a man who breaks all constraints.
    He has been bolted in, riveted in, tied with
    wet sheets, bound in straitjackets, in the hospitals.
    We played all the towns.
    (The scene opens to a grove of evergreens. HOUDINI *and*
    BEATRICE *walk over the maroon-colors of fallen pine needles.*
    Slant shafts of light. Three gravestones: a tall Celtic cross and
    two small stones, one on each side.)

HOUDINI
    A tank town in the sticks.
    A walk in the country.

BEATRICE
    Smell the clover. Harry, the fresh-cut grass.

HOUDINI
    All right, Marco. Volonty's gone to the beauty shop. Go find
    a massage parlor.

MARCO BONE
    Two minutes, boss.
    (Exits.)

BEATRICE

They're good, working alone or together. They can find out enough in two or three hours so that we can run a flawless mind-reading act tonight.

HOUDINI

If you help me, too. Bess—you flashed out at me as I came out of the ice. Beyond belief, and I know. Terror and waiting, for you. But I know *in myself* I can get through. All the escapes!

BEATRICE

Terror of what I knew you were seeing.

HOUDINI

When I had almost forgotten how to breathe, memory,
like a diagram of ice and air. There, under any
ice, I remembered, a layer of air. I lay back
in the water, just under that hard ceiling,
letting my lungs fill. That small space, that
last-minute breath gave me a second chance.
I could come home to you.

BEATRICE

I thought you had gone.
When did you first know?

HOUDINI

On the beach, when you spoke about magic. It meant Bess and me, joined.

BEATRICE

In bed, on the stage?

HOUDINI

Yes. Help me with these stones.

BEATRICE

Volonty in the beauty parlor, collecting gossip; Marco in the whorehouse, collecting names and intimate details. And our afternoon in the green woods—

HOUDINI

(Bent over the base of the Celtic cross.)
What do you think this one is?

BEATRICE

A father and two children? No.

HOUDINI

Well, this is a woman with a very long life. Frances Strang. And the children?

BEATRICE

Not exactly children. "Mitchell Strang, beloved husband of —" and his dates.

HOUDINI

(At the other small stone.)
This is beloved husband too. What have you got? Mine is ten years later.

BEATRICE

It's their private plot, Harry. Ah, we'll read their minds tonight. It's surely the grand estate of the town. And these are the people behind it, information. Wife; they're not children, they're husbands.

HOUDINI

Bess—you think it's all escapes for me. Something holds me to you, past—I can't say past what. But you do more than hold me. You are far, and leading me. And Moses and Jesus do their transformations.

BEATRICE

It's your eyes, Harry, your body, Harry, yourself, what you show me.

HOUDINI

Your moving—the actual magic. What I do can be reasoned out, I work with the sciences and the limits of the watcher, who thinks he sees. This spruce tree in summer, that lasts beyond summer.

BEATRICE

What would happen if one woman told the truth about her life? The world would split open.

HOUDINI

It has. Now I'm going after it—all pieces.

HOUDINI *(Song: "I Make My Magic")*
    I MAKE MY MAGIC
    OF FORGOTTEN THINGS:
    NIGHT AND NIGHTMARE AND THE MIDNIGHT WINGS
    OF CHILDHOOD BUTTERFLIES—
    AND THE DARKNESS, THE STRAINING DARK
    UNDERWATER AND UNDER SLEEP—
    NIGHT AND A HEARTBREAK TRY TO KEEP
    MYSELF, UNTIL BEFORE MY EYES
    THE MORNING SUNLIGHT POURS

AND I AM CLEAR OF ALL THE CHAINS
AND THE MAGIC NOW THAT RAINS
DOWN AROUND ME IS
A SUNLIGHT MAGIC,
I COME TO A SUNLIGHT MAGIC,
YOURS.

(Flip of scene. HOUDINI *and* MARCO BONE.*)*

MARCO BONE

All right, Harry. You got her out of the circus, you said you had plans for her.

HOUDINI

Nothing has ever used what Volonty has.

MARCO BONE

I can use it.

HOUDINI

Who couldn't? But there's more. She can wiggle her ass, and she can use everything she's got, but there's more than that — her questions, too. Let's take that offer from London.

MARCO BONE

—Ah, that will really do it, Harry! With an escape, and a Disappearing Woman, and a show-'em-up séance — it's Bess for the disappearance, isn't it?

HOUDINI

For the moment, yes. She wants it. But not for long. Look for a new one.

MARCO BONE

Harry. It's not good there, is it? If I can ask.

HOUDINI

Yes, it's good. Yes, ask.

MARCO BONE

It's not good in bed, Harry? That's what I think. No offense.

HOUDINI

Well, it's past anything, as it happens, Marco, more than ever. But there is something.

MARCO BONE

What else is there?

HOUDINI

No matter what's around, Marco. It's Bess. And it will always be Bess. And nobody else. No child, I mean. You don't say anything.

MARCO BONE

That's not what I'm about, Harry. I can't even see that it makes all that much difference. Or even much of any difference.

HOUDINI

It does to Bess. You know her little poodle? That's where it is by now. Gathered together, swinging on a trapeze.

MARCO BONE

   I would put it plainer than that.
   —And your mother?

HOUDINI

   I haven't told her that I really know by now. But I want to
   tell her. I want really to ask her.

MARCO BONE

   She's in it very much for you, Harry?

HOUDINI

   A child—for me to go on, for her to go on.

MARCO BONE

   Wouldn't you adopt one?

HOUDINI

   No, I don't think so.

MARCO BONE

   Or you have one with somebody? Or Bess likewise? And say
   nothing? Keeping the child?
   (HOUDINI *swings on him.*)
   What does your mother say, then?

HOUDINI

   I haven't told her, I said. Maybe I could write it better. Maybe
   when we go to Europe, I could write it to her. Or send a
   record and talk to her. But it doesn't make any difference be-
   tween Bess and me. Fact. It may make things better. All,
   completely, between the two of us.

ACT TWO, SCENE TWO

MARCO BONE

He has been bolted in, riveted in; he has been laced in, tied with tarred ropes and wet sheets, locked in a government mail pouch. He has been hanged, upside down.

VOLONTY

And he has escaped, every time.

MARCO BONE

In Massachusetts once, he made his way out of a dead whale.

VOLONTY

Take a letter to Jonah.

MARCO BONE

Have you seen him tossed into the harbor in a box, the tugboat standing by? Have you seen him disappear the elephant, or swallow yards and yards of threaded needles? Have you seen him diving into all the rivers?

VOLONTY

I have something else: the man who has to escape.

MARCO BONE

And I have seen them worship him. He says it to them. He breaks the handcuffs, and they know something about free; they sit there shaking; they wait on windy street corners while he wriggles, fast, hard, and gets himself out of his constraint.

VOLONTY

Heard what Bernhardt did? Sarah Bernhardt? She waited for him in her car; when he came out of the water, she asked him to go for a drive. Turned to him in the car and said, "Houdini, you're the only man who can do it. Give me back my leg . . ." Among the poor and mad. Three-hundred pairs of shoes for poor boys, in a town in Scotland. He leaps from wing to wing of planes. But most with the soldiers. "They have been buried alive," he says.
(The whole stage opens to the Houdini Show. At audience left, we see a part of the wings, HOUDINI *doing his limbering exercises and practicing contortionist contractions.)*

MARCO BONE and BEATRICE   *(Song: "What the King Said")*
TODAY YOUR AMBASSADOR SAID IN FUN,
"THINGS ARE TOUGH IN WASHINGTON —
LET'S GO SEE WHAT HOUDINI HAS DONE."
WITH ALL THE FORMS OF AMERICAN RAPE,
WE NEED A GOOD ALL-PURPOSE ESCAPE,
    AN ALL-PURPOSE GOOD ECONOMY ESCAPE . . .
EVERY PRESIDENT AND KING
MUST BE ABLE TO GET OUT OF EVERYTHING,
    SO DO IT 'N' DO IT 'N' DO IT 'N' DO IT HOUDINI,
    DO DO DO IT FOR ME.

His Majesty said to Houdini the Great:
"Just the thing for a head of state,
You can have all your locks and clocks
As long as I'm in the royal box;
I've too much sense to investigate.

    Do it as long as I can see,
From the orchestra or the balcony,
And all the princesses agree

    Whatever it is you do Houdini
    Do it 'n' do it 'n' do it 'n' do it for me —
    Except for the wildest youngest of all
        princesses
    And she sings rapturously:
    Do it 'n' do it 'n' do it 'n' do it Houdini,
    Do do do it to me."

HOUDINI

This is an occasion. This is the farewell performance of my wife, Mrs. Houdini.
(The phone rings.)

VOLONTY

Hello. Yes, this is the Houdini Show. I'm afraid I can't call him. Oh. Just a minute. Bess! Long distance. I'm sorry, Bess, it's very bad news.

BEATRICE

(Enters from offstage.)
Yes. Yes. Harry!

HOUDINI

Is it mother?
(He takes the phone.)

This is Harry Houdini. Yes, yes. In the middle of saying what? Did anyone else hear what she said? What did it sound like? Repeat the first part. Yes. Yes. Of course you are.
(He hangs up.)
They couldn't understand what she was saying. She tried to talk to me, she was saying something for me when she died: "Tell Harry..." All right, Marco, pay off the whole company. We're leaving for New York tonight.

MARCO BONE

All right. Let's go. Let's go.

VOLONTY

He knew, when the phone rang. When I lost my child, some kind of horror came to me again and again. It kept bleeding into the next place. I threw myself on seeing everything.

MARCO BONE

I know, with you. Volonty.

VOLONTY

You know some things. And your name begins with an "M."

MARCO BONE

No it doesn't. I'm John Doe, found in a basket in a drugstore doorway when I was four weeks old. I invented Marco Bone. And I know what you want, Volonty.

VOLONTY

All I want is to stay with the show. But I begin to see you.

HOUDINI
(Black suspenders, his sign of mourning. To BEATRICE.*)*
Do you think it was about me?

BEATRICE
Of course it was.

VOLONTY
Marco, if you could do anything, what would it be?

MARCO BONE
Something with you in it, baby. And the shooting gallery.
Targets that nobody's ever seen.

VOLONTY
I'd do something I've never done.

MARCO BONE
What's that?

VOLONTY
I don't know. Something I'd wake up with long ago. I was
following something or somebody, coursing over long
roads —

MARCO BONE
Sounds like a fox hunt.

VOLONTY
No, I hate that. But some kind of running. Bodiless.

MARCO BONE

You go on asking your questions. And maybe, let go of Houdini.

HOUDINI

I must have that word. No. Don't comfort me. She was going to tell me—

BEATRICE

What?

HOUDINI

I must.

BEATRICE

Yes.

HOUDINI

I guess it's a matter of hope. Like anything else. I must hope.

BEATRICE

(*She is afraid now.*)
Of course, you must.

HOUDINI

If I knew that word . . . Who can find it? Who can hear?

BEATRICE

There are many ways of hearing, Harry.

HOUDINI

There are many ways of speaking, Bess.

BEATRICE
Spilling acid, for one?
(They laugh together.)

HOUDINI
What do you smell?

BEATRICE
The sea.

HOUDINI
What else?

BEATRICE
Wicker furniture. My perfume. An expensive hotel room.

HOUDINI
What else?

BEATRICE
Nothing. We're too high up.

MARCO BONE
And now he needs a guide, the ruler of this kingdom.
(CONAN DOYLE *and* LADY DOYLE, *sitting side by side — the king and queen of this side of life.)*
Houdini is out in the whistling winds of this storm, and he knows that for him it is the kingdom of madness. All his life he has imitated séances, making the faces appear — here comes your father's spirit and your unborn child. But now he comes to the wise man and woman, and he is their child. He runs to them. It is Conan Doyle and Lady Doyle. Sir

99

Arthur Conan Doyle can be trusted. He is honest beyond question. He is rational beyond question. He is the man who wrote the Sherlock Holmes stories, who created Sherlock Holmes—pure reason and deduction. Much more than that, Conan Doyle is in the great world and the afterworld. His wife is a famous medium; they have been able to reach their son . . .

CONAN DOYLE

We have been able to reach our son, who was killed in the Great War.

MARCO BONE

That's World War I. They called it the World War, although only a few countries were involved. Like the World Series. But many men were killed, and many families went to séances afterward.

LADY DOYLE

Happiness! After you've been searching so long. Our boy spoke to me—so clear, so fine, as he was in life, but only to my sight, only to sound.

CONAN DOYLE

Houdini is a skeptic, but everything he does these days is a signal for help.

LADY DOYLE

We won't let that poor Mr. Houdini go searching another minute.

CONAN DOYLE

Of course we'll help. We're in Atlantic City, and they've been sporting on the sand with our young children. They'll have their séance. He'll speak to his mother. I know it.
(The HOUDINIs *again, locked in their fight.)*

BEATRICE

Harry? Many ways of being: the boy who spilled acid on my dress, the wild man Borneo, the grown man breaking out of every conceivable bond . . . they're just masks, aren't they?

HOUDINI

What are you trying to do to me?

BEATRICE

You're hanging on a word from your dead mother!

HOUDINI

You greedy bitch.

BEATRICE

Bitch I am, greedy I am.

HOUDINI

You want me to reach only you.

BEATRICE

Yes, I want you to reach me.

HOUDINI

Only one trick there.

BEATRICE

No trick!

HOUDINI

I prepare myself for illusions. I have to prepare myself for the real, too.

BEATRICE

What do you mean?

HOUDINI

Prepare yourself! Be there for me when I come to you. Don't fade away, don't disappear.

BEATRICE

You come to me in the same fierce way all the time . . . that I could love if it were only one of the *many* ways of making love. Harry . . . I invent the rope trick.

HOUDINI

It's been invented.

BEATRICE

No, this is the real rope trick. You look out at them in your marvelous way, and go up the rope, out of sight, and I follow you and pull the rope up after me. No, the rope follows me.

HOUDINI

And what happens? What happens, Bess?

BEATRICE

We make love . . . just out of reach . . . out of sight of everybody.

HOUDINI

Get off my back, Bess. You just want to get back in the act.

BEATRICE

I don't think you're going to get that word, Harry. Ever.

HOUDINI

You know who you find up in the sky at the end of that rope? Houdini, stark mad. More than in the river, deeper than underground when it all gave way to panic, here comes the vast wave, Bess . . . This is the thing I always said drove people to madness. And I crawl to it, I rush to it—

BEATRICE

Don't go, Harry! This once, stay with me, love me, don't go. You could always call me back from great distances. Don't risk madness here.

HOUDINI

I am moving now, racing with the speed of darkness, and you stand still.

BEATRICE

I have seen you stand on the wings of planes.
(A bell rings.)

HOUDINI

They are waiting for us.
(They are in the séance chamber.)

HOUDINI

You know, I have never believed.

CONAN DOYLE

But your mind is open.

HOUDINI

My mind is open. I'm willing to believe, but I have never seen . . .

CONAN DOYLE

We are aware that you can produce what the false mediums show. But we are not false. And many people can do wonders, once they've been done. Look what athletes can do, once the record is broken! We are not false.

HOUDINI

I know you aren't. And if this could happen — if this could really come true to me, I think my whole life would be changed.

LADY DOYLE

And you do have hope, dear boy?

HOUDINI

Yes, I have hope . . .

LADY DOYLE

I should like to begin.

CONAN DOYLE

Is that agreeable to you, dear fellow?

HOUDINI

It's a relief to be with friends. Let's, by all means, go ahead. *(He sits down and is finally very still.)*

LADY DOYLE

> Splendid. Here are my pencils ... sharp ... and the paper.
> You may examine everything. Here, my dear. If there is writ-
> ing, you understand, it will not be I who writes. Sometimes
> there is a voice. The voice will not be mine. And no bangings,
> no tambourines, no "spook stuff." We are here in devotion
> and simplicity. Yes. Will you say the final words, Arthur?

CONAN DOYLE

> Let us place our hands on the table. Almighty Lord, in
> whom all things are spirit, allow us to achieve the spirit.
> Vouchsafe us to know the communion of souls across all bar-
> riers, space, time, and death. That communion which makes
> us part of Thee. Grant that our hearts may be answered. And
> our search. Thy will be done.
> (*A wait.*)

LADY DOYLE

> Arthur, perhaps the last light out.

CONAN DOYLE

> Of course.
> (*Another wait.*)

LADY DOYLE

> I'm sorry, but there does seem to be an unfavorable influence
> in the room. Perhaps if we could hold the séance without it,
> we might hope for excellent results.
> (*No one says anything, or moves.*)

BEATRICE

> I'll be in my room, Harry.

(*She leaves.* HOUDINI *does not move.* LADY DOYLE'*s pencil suddenly beats on the table. A tremor goes through her.* HOUDINI *starts up to help her.*)

CONAN DOYLE
No! Leave her be.

(HOUDINI *subsides and sits stone still during the séance, frozen as we have never seen him. The contact of hands has been broken. But now the pencil is touching the table before* LADY DOYLE. *Her tremor is violent, not rhythmical, but productive; it begins to make marks on the paper.*

Séance Music. Single notes of music are heard, a chromatic music related to the River Music at the end of ACT ONE. *As the writing begins, cloud shapes form in the air over the table. The pencil is luminous. It makes the sign of the cross on the paper before* LADY DOYLE.)

HOUDINI
A cross?

CONAN DOYLE
The messages begin this way.
(*He tears the paper away as she forms big letters on the sheets. Nothing is rhythmical.*)

LADY DOYLE
(*In a strange voice.*)
Thank God I am through to you. My darling.
I am with you today and always.
A happiness awaits you that you dreamed of as a child.

Do not grieve for the evidence you need.
I am in the blessed fields, grass-green, silver-green, blissful-
    green.
(*The cloud forms take the shape of river monsters, circus
people, like the Goya painting of the Fates. From now on*
HOUDINI *is locked in a memory of the world under the river.*)
And I long for you, my darling boy . . . to be happy.
You have brought us together. We must . . . write.
Farewell . . .
(*In her own voice.*)
Did anything come through?

CONAN DOYLE

It was marvelous. Direct communication.

LADY DOYLE

I am so glad. And extremely tired. If you will excuse me . . .
(*She goes.*)

ENSEMBLE   (*Song: "Floating Figures"*)
        VISIONS, POWERS, DOMINATIONS, FEAR.
        AND THE RABBI DANCED,
        AND THE MAGICIAN SANG,
        AND ALL THE ECHOES OF THE ECHOES RANG
        DOWN CENTURIES OF RAIN,
        DOWN MILES OF TEARS.
        THE YEARS . . . THE MAKING LOVE . . .
        THE BELIEF . . . THE YEARS . . .
        VISIONS . . .
        POWERS . . .
        DOMINATIONS . . .
        FEARS . . .

HOUDINI
I wanted to . . .

CONAN DOYLE
(Assuming everything.)
We are very happy for you.

HOUDINI
I wanted to be in touch with her —

CONAN DOYLE
It was so clear. You felt her presence in this room, didn't you?

HOUDINI
Not her voice. Not her language. She didn't use English like that. She made the sign of the cross —

CONAN DOYLE
We change in life, and afterward.

HOUDINI
She never called me "darling." She knew I had bad dreams as a child, all bad dreams; I hardly slept. Today was her birthday; she would have mentioned that. The whole arrangement that is a person —

CONAN DOYLE
But all your changed people, fragmented, the moon for their heads —

HOUDINI

Those are illusions that speak to us. Tricks! Technical!

CONAN DOYLE

A minute ago, you had what you wanted.

HOUDINI

(Breaking. In a dead voice.)
It would have meant life to me.

CONAN DOYLE

The responsibility of accepting or rejecting is with you. It is a very real responsibility.

HOUDINI

I know it is your religion —

CONAN DOYLE

You doubt, after what you have heard?
This is insanity!
(The apparitions vanish when HOUDINI *lunges for* CONAN DOYLE'*s throat. A great flurry of the papers, they fly up in a white snowstorm in front of a huge bull's-eye light, snow in front of a locomotive.* HOUDINI *cannot attack* CONAN DOYLE. *He picks up his chair and slams it down in splinters at* CONAN DOYLE'*s feet.)*

HOUDINI

Lost. She is lost.
Bess is lost to me.
Jamie who ran away with me; the locomotive killed him.
(The big light goes out.)

CONAN DOYLE
Use your loss!

HOUDINI
What my what?

CONAN DOYLE
Does Sarah Bernhardt talk to her leg? Volonty sing lullabies to her dead child?

HOUDINI
(*Jeering* CONAN DOYLE's *other creation.*)
Ah, Doctor Watson! I'll fight you to the end, Arthur!

CONAN DOYLE
I'm your friend forever.

HOUDINI
You can talk to the dead, but the dead won't talk to you. Fakes!

CONAN DOYLE
They say you're the king of fakes, Harry.

HOUDINI
I tell them I'm deceiving them. The public begs for these . . . optical illusions. I give them entertainment. Do they see what they believe? Do they believe what they see? I'll show them up, every last one!

CONAN DOYLE
You don't understand yourself.

HOUDINI

Understand! I chalk their hands, cut their threads, grease their fraudulent trumpets —

CONAN DOYLE

And Lady Doyle's pencil?

HOUDINI

*(To the tune of "*ROSABELLE.*")*
"Over me you . . . cast your spell . . ."
Talk to the dead. They won't talk to you. Something's rational here, with all the irrational. I'm going to Bess.
(They leave separately, in hostility. A moment of quiet; and then the real emanation appears, a witty, angular, recognizable figure in his cap, pipe in teeth, a tap-dancer.)

VOLONTY

(Announcing.)
You know him, and he's not Doctor Watson. Everybody! The real creation of Conan Doyle, the detective of detectives!

SHERLOCK HOLMES and VOLONTY

(Song: "When Mr. Holmes Goes Into His Dance")
>NEVER MIND YOUR PENCIL
>NEVER MIND YOUR TRANCE
>EVERYTHING IS RATIONAL
>YOU KNOW IN ADVANCE —
>GOOD-BYE HALLUCINATION,
>HELLO, SECOND CHANCE —
>>WHODUNIT, HOUDINI?
>>WHEN MR. HOLMES GOES INTO HIS DANCE!

(They exit.)

BEATRICE
 (Alone.)
 Bess of loneliness.
 Bess of sorrow.
 (Pure self-pity. But then she begins to sing, pouring out her real answer to everything that has happened—melting aria, an appeal that is something like a spiritual, a cadenza of all the old hurt and her new imperviousness, and finally, gut-bucket. Her answer is profusion.)

BEATRICE, HOUDINI, VOLONTY, MARCO BONE,
and ENSEMBLE   *(Song: "Beatrice's Song Cycle")*

BEATRICE

    ALONE AND KNOWING HOW ALONE I AM
    UNTIL THE CHAMPAGNE GIRLS
    EMERGE AND SING.
    WHILE HE WAITS. I HAVE WAITED,
    TOO LONG, TOO LONG,
    TO COME TO SONG.

    LORD, MAKE ME STRONG,
    GIVE ME MY SONG AGAIN,
    LORD, MAKE ME WISE,
    GIVE ME MY EYES AGAIN,
    GIVE ME HIS EYES, GIVE HIM HIS EYES,
    GIVE US OUR EYES.

    WHAT CAN HIS MOTHER DO?
    WHAT CAN HIS MOTHER SAY?
    FOR GOD'S SAKE, HARRY, LIVE!
    FOR GOD'S SAKE, BESS!
    WHAT CAN HIS MOTHER DO?

WHAT KIND OF GIRL DID HE BRING HOME?
WHAT KIND OF GIRL DID HE BRING HOME?

ROSABELLE, MY ROSABELLE,
I LOVE YOU MORE THAN I CAN TELL —
OVER ME YOU CAST A SPELL —
I LOVE YOU, MY SWEET ROSABELLE

LET ME SEE,
LET ME FEEL,
LET ME KNOW WHAT IS REAL,
LET ME BELIEVE . . .

MOMMA? . . .
MOMMA, I WANT MY MAGIC MAN,
NOT THE OLD SHUT-OUT KIND,
MOMMA, I WANT MY MAGIC MAN,
NOT A MAN WHO IS BLIND.

A BLIND MAN SEES A WOMAN
(*Enter* HOUDINI.)
BY FEEL, BY FEEL —
HE BLINDS HIMSELF — IT'S HUMAN,
BUT THAT MAKES HIM UNREAL.

MOMMA, I GOT A DEATHY MAN,
MAKE HIM PART OF MY LIFE,
MOMMA, I WANT MY MAGIC MAN
SO I CAN BE A WOMAN,
BE A WOMAN,
BE A WIFE.
(*Pause, alone.*)

113

HOUDINI

> BE A WOMAN, BE A WOMAN,
> WITHOUT ANYTHING, BE . . .

> AND, THEN, THEN,
> BE A WIFE.
> *(Enter* ENTIRE COMPANY.*)*

VOLONTY and MARCO BONE

> BE A WOMAN, BE A WOMAN, BE A WIFE.

ENSEMBLE

> MOMMA, I WANT MY MAGIC MAN,
> SO I CAN BE A WOMAN, BE A WOMAN, BE A WIFE.
> *(Exit all but* VOLONTY *and* MARCO BONE.*)*

VOLONTY

So I found my new vocation. The high-wire dancer, stripper, body fortune-teller, she finds she has something else than Sherlock Holmes —

MARCO BONE

All right, beautiful, just the announcements.

VOLONTY

There's more to it than that.

MARCO BONE

Everything you do is an announcement.

ACT TWO, SCENE THREE

(MARCO BONE, *far down on the stage;* VOLONTY *on the other side.)*

MARCO BONE
> He fought for the word from his mother. He
> met false hope. He fought false hope.
>
> This man is no Galileo, no Einstein, no Freud.
> This man is a lock breaker, name of Houdini.

VOLONTY
> Houdini escapes, every time.

MARCO BONE
> But he didn't pick the lock of that last door.
> He broke the door down.
> And now escape is an empty lock behind him.

VOLONTY
> Now he needs to find.

MARCO BONE
> And you know what happens then.
> You just may get yourself invited to Washington.
>
> It can happen.
> Sometimes in your own bedroom, watching the news.
> This time, it's a more formal invitation.
> To a more formal place.

VOLONTY
> (*In a big, amplified voice.*)
> Houdini, you know the ropes! Come and testify!

HOUDINI
> (*Enters with* BEATRICE.)
> Well, sure. There's no rush, is there?
> And give me a few pointers.
> I've never been in a courtroom.

VOLONTY and MARCO BONE
> He's never been in a courtroom.

BEATRICE
> Well, there's no risk. He's not on trial.

VOLONTY
> There's always a risk. Not just at trials.
> The man can call you on the carpet.
> Questions can pour in under your door.
> And this is a hearing. A congressional hearing.

HOUDINI
> On magic?

MARCO BONE
Fortune-telling. Same difference.
Still willing to testify?

HOUDINI
Well, of course.
My whole life's been leading to this.

BEATRICE
I don't see that at all.

HOUDINI
There's a bill—

VOLONTY
What's a bill?

MARCO BONE
One team is trying to pass a law against fortune-telling.

SPECTATOR
No fortune-telling? Why should he do magic and me not do
fortunes?

SPECTATOR
Quien sabe.

SPECTATOR
No capish.

SPECTATOR
Ish kabibble.

HOUDINI
> Don't worry, darling. I'm not on trial.

VOLONTY
> Well, they've asked you to come in now.

MARCO BONE
> A small boy begins in. They get in, somehow.

BOY
> *(A reminder of* HOUDINI *at twelve.)*
> Mr. Houdini . . . can I have a quarter?

HOUDINI
> Sure . . . Here, I'll show you something.
> *(Slowly.)*
> Bim. Bam. Boozle.
> *(He hands the* BOY *a coin.)*
> You try . . . no. See it? . . . now faster. Don't watch the coin.
> Watch the fingers. Bimbamboozle. Got it?

BOY
> Got it!

HOUDINI
> That's better than just a quarter, hey? You can make —
> *(His hand on the* BOY's *head. The hearing chamber. It has a
> resemblance to the shooting gallery at Coney Island.)*

MARCO BONE
> This is the bill, 8989. It's against anybody telling fortunes for

money, or being paid for card tricks and con games, or pretending to remove spells—he or she shall be considered a thief and a blackmailer and shall be punished.

SPECTATOR
No fortune-telling in the White House?

BEATRICE
(*Sitting behind* HOUDINI.)
But how could your profession come into this?

HOUDINI
I don't know, but if it is—

BEATRICE
I swear, Harry . . . if you . . .

HOUDINI
You'll leave me?
(*Kisses her.*)

FIRST CONGRESSMAN
This hearing is convened.

SECOND CONGRESSMAN
I would like Mr. Houdini to make a statement, as a key witness.

THIRD CONGRESSMAN
May I inquire who he is?

FIRST CONGRESSMAN
Call Houdini.
Mr. Chairman! This is my bill. I move that Houdini be heard.
(HOUDINI *takes the stand.*)
What is your full name.

HOUDINI
Harry Houdini.

VARICK
The original Houdini was a Hindu, wasn't he?
Answer yes or no.

HOUDINI
No.

VARICK
Are you Houdini the second?

HOUDINI
No.

VARICK
Are you the original Houdini?

HOUDINI
You're thinking of Houdin, the Frenchman that I took my
name from.

SPECTATOR
Took something from a Frenchman!

VARICK

I thought he lived in Allahabad.

HOUDINI

Are you joking?

VARICK

No, I am in earnest.

HOUDINI

His name was Robert Houdin. He was a trick master, and I exposed him in a book I've written.

SPECTATOR

Exposed your ancestor!

SPECTATOR

Ripped the clothes off his granddaddy!

VARICK

Just answer yes or no.

HOUDINI

My name is Houdini.

CONGRESSMAN

And your real name?

HOUDINI

My real name is Harry Houdini, by the law of the United States of America many years ago.

VARICK

Wasn't your original name Weiss?

HOUDINI

I was born under that name.

VARICK

Have you ever been to Allahabad?

HOUDINI

Never in my life.

VARICK

Have you ever read the Arabian Nights stories?

HOUDINI

Yes, sir.

VARICK

But you have never been there?

GILBERT

Were both your parents Jewish?

HOUDINI

Yes, they were.

GILBERT

You're against the resurrection, aren't you?
Isn't that why you're against mediums?

HOUDINI

I am not attacking religion. I respect any genuine believer in any religion. But this thing they call spiritualism, talking with the dead, is a fraud. I have not seen one genuine medium. And it's an American art, you know. It started here, we're responsible for it.

CONGRESSMAN

You've been fighting them, Mr. Houdini. Are you successful?

HOUDINI

More mediums have been arrested through me in the last two years than in the 70 before.

SPECTATOR

Mr. Houdini's rotten work! I'm not a gypsy queen, I'm the science of the future! He's trying to destroy others, and Houdini is destroying himself. Mr. Houdini has placed so many people mentally in the asylum that his thought may return to him and place him there . . .

HOUDINI

No, I have walked through that; it's part of me now.

CONGRESSMAN

I believe in Santa Claus! No disrespect from the press!

CONGRESSMAN

Is it true, Mr. Houdini, that you're the head of a secret organization?

HOUDINI
Society of American Magicians. Only secret about our exploits.

CONGRESSMAN
What is your business?

HOUDINI
I am a writer. I am a psychic investigator, and I perform stage illusions.

CONGRESSMAN
You don't claim special powers?

HOUDINI
No, sir, I am human.

SPIRITUALIST
Conan Doyle says he has supernatural powers.

CONGRESSMAN
What do you say to that?

HOUDINI
I deny it.

CONGRESSMAN
Can you prove it?

HOUDINI
I *admit* that I am human.

CONGRESSMAN
But Conan Doyle is one of the greatest authorities . . .

HOUDINI
No, sir, he is a dupe. He believes what he wants to believe.

CONGRESSMAN
I have heard you can fly through keyholes.

HOUDINI
Many people will tell you they see—whatever I've wanted them to see. They're not able to describe what has happened. They'll accept what you seem to show them, if they don't know the laws of science, or the laws of belief. True belief is a great thing, I care about that. My father wrote a book—

CONGRESSMAN
Is Mr. Houdini a mystic?

SPIRITUALIST
Mr. Houdini is one of the greatest mystics in the world.

CONGRESSMAN
You say it's—just magic?

HOUDINI
Yes. I simply have not explained some of it.

CONGRESSMAN
Not to anyone?

HOUDINI
Not to my dearest friends.

CONGRESSMAN
Does this hearing apply to spiritualism?

HOUDINI
Under the guise of spiritualism, they tell fortunes.
(*Imitates.*)
There's a large head coming towards me.
(*His hands reach out.*)
I see a woman scolding a child. "Shame! Shame!" The child is covering his eyes. That's their way of telling things; it's a way we recognize; that's the way we tell our dreams, in the present, but that's the continual present of creation. Now these people, in many towns they get the women alone and put their hands all over their bodies. They tell you how to win back your lover. They tell you about love. And they do it under the cloak of religion.

VARICK
Are you attacking religion? Answer yes or no.

HOUDINI
No.

CONGRESSMAN
Are you attacking lovers?

CONGRESSMAN
Are you attacking bodies?

HOUDINI
No. I speak through the body.

MARCO BONE

In a great medical school, three students, late at night, are going over the long lists of the parts of the body. They are going through their long exercises, as if they were acrobats in training, concentrating, putting themselves through their long, painful hours. Not so painful? They have their own ideas about what the body is.

(Change of scene. Room in a medical school. THREE MEDICAL STUDENTS, *sharply differentiated by hair color and movement. The actors are the three clowns of the circus scene.)*

FIRST MEDICAL STUDENT

(Slams a huge, heavy anatomy book, throws it.)
God, I can't. I can't get these straight. I can't even see straight.

SECOND MEDICAL STUDENT

Can't what?

FIRST MEDICAL STUDENT

It's this goddamn memorization. I can't do the cranial nerves.

SECOND MEDICAL STUDENT

The facial nerves?

FIRST MEDICAL STUDENT

Optic, olfactory, oculomotor. What comes next?

THIRD MEDICAL STUDENT

Get a grip. Morose, half-dead —

FIRST MEDICAL STUDENT

Morose! I'm in some dream. Medical students! I'm asleep with all the lights on. Endless work, drilling. *That* can't be the body — what I saw in the lab today, a cadaver with the top of the skull lifted out, a tear rolling out of her eye — and these nerves, optic, olfactory, then what?

SECOND MEDICAL STUDENT

How can I draw with you yammering? Here, you know how to remember those nerves: On Old Olympus's / Towering Tops / A Finn and German / Picked Some Hops.

FIRST MEDICAL STUDENT

What the hell are you saying?

SECOND MEDICAL STUDENT

It's the initials, fool.
On Old Olympus — Optic, Olfactory, Oculomotor
Towering Tops — Trochlear, Trigeminal
A Finn and German — Abducens, Facial, Acoustic, Glosso-
   pharyngeal
Picked Some Hops — Pneumogaftrac, Spinal, Hypoglossal
That's beer. That's what I want. For a chaser.
I want a boilermaker.

FIRST MEDICAL STUDENT

On Old Lympus's — Optic, Olfactory, Oculomotor —
(Touching his eye, nose, eye.)

SECOND MEDICAL STUDENT

Oculomotor — that's what it takes in this portrait — look it's the way Houdini holds his eyes wide, hypnotizing you. I did this from a newspaper picture. But he says he'll sit for me when he's here.

THIRD MEDICAL STUDENT
That's not the verse. That's kid stuff. Let's see the picture.
(*Looks at the picture.*)
Who's Houdini?

SECOND MEDICAL STUDENT
He's playing the next stage show at the Bijou.

THIRD MEDICAL STUDENT
Oh, the clown.

SECOND MEDICAL STUDENT
He's no clown, he's a magician.
A magus.

FIRST MEDICAL STUDENT
What do you mean, kid stuff?

THIRD MEDICAL STUDENT
Well, what we say is —

FIRST MEDICAL STUDENT
No, I really don't know.

THIRD MEDICAL STUDENT
O O O to Touch And Feel A Girl's Vagina And Hymen.

FIRST MEDICAL STUDENT
O O O To Touch And Feel —

SECOND MEDICAL STUDENT
I'd rather find a woman and get drunk.

FIRST MEDICAL STUDENT
How can it be Vagina And Hymen if the other rhyme says
Picked Some Hops?

THIRD MEDICAL STUDENT
Well, it's Vagus, Accessory, Hypoglossal. Like your vagus
magus. And you can remember them this way, can't you?

FIRST MEDICAL STUDENT
(Repeating.)
O O O To Touch And Feel—A Girl's Vagina And Hymen—

THIRD MEDICAL STUDENT
You won't ever forget that.
God, I need a woman! I should never have broken with my
girl. But what else was there to do?
Let's go out, for God's sake.
Aren't you coming.

SECOND MEDICAL STUDENT
I want to take this drawing further. I can't seem to get that
look of his into it.

THIRD MEDICAL STUDENT
Ah, let it go till you see him.
Let's get out of the charnel house.

FIRST MEDICAL STUDENT
Why do you call Houdini a clown? What are you?

THIRD MEDICAL STUDENT

Well, a monkey dressed up! Hocus pocus, kiss my tocus. We're going to heal people. What the hell, you know those nerves now, don't you? Come on. On the town. You know enough not to let yourself rot in this nightmare with the light on?

(*Exit* MEDICAL STUDENTS.)

MARCO BONE

At the hearing, in Washington, Houdini says he is not attacking bodies.

HOUDINI

I am attacking fraud. These mediums—they drive people to madness, to the hospitals. They call on survivors to join their loved ones; after they've made their wills in favor of the medium, they're driven to suicide.

CONGRESSMAN

You deny a boy and a girl at a fair a little fun?

HOUDINI

A little heroin, a little opium. Just enough to make him happy.

CONGRESSMAN

Can you show us a test of any of this?

HOUDINI

I'll make you an offer: $10,000 to anyone who can read my mind.

(*Silence.*)

What did my mother call me when I was a child.
(*Silence.*)
Who taught me the rope trick?
(*Silence. He takes a piece of paper, crumples it, throws it on the floor.*)
Read that, any of you, show me up!
All right, another challenge. Anybody! Come up and hit me
     as hard as you want.
(*Man comes forward, socks him;* HOUDINI *is braced, and takes it smiling.*)

SPECTATOR

That's not the mind.

HOUDINI

The body is part of the mind. That offer stands.

SPECTATOR

He's a fake. Send for Grattan. He knew him when.

VOLONTY

Grattan can't come.

SPECTATORS

Who's he? The circus man? To show up Houdini — he's got
to come, if he's called.

VOLONTY

He can't. He got his lion, and the lion tore the poor guy's arm
off.

MARCO BONE

In this business you're bound to lose something.

CONGRESSMAN
Don't you know sorrow, Houdini? Haven't you ever wanted consolation? Answer yes or no.

HOUDINI
Yes.

CONGRESSMAN
Call Sir Arthur Conan Doyle.

VOLONTY
He doesn't have to appear.

CONGRESSMAN
He wants to.
(CONAN DOYLE *takes the stand.*)

CONAN DOYLE
Yes, he has powers greater than human powers.

HOUDINI
I swear I don't.

CONAN DOYLE
I don't even know how you got out of that diving suit.

HOUDINI
Everything was by ordinary means!

CONAN DOYLE
The whole thing beats me completely.

HOUDINI
Help me stand up against this corrupt and fraudulent thing.

CONAN DOYLE
I know you want to do that, Harry. But help the mediums.

HOUDINI
You're asking me to do the impossible.

CONAN DOYLE
Yes, but you do the impossible.

HOUDINI
I *admit* I do not.

CONGRESSMAN
The gentleman's time has expired.

HOUDINI
May I call my investigators?

CONGRESSMAN
You may call your first witness.

SPECTATORS
Mouth, nose, anus, eyes, he says he's here to stop thieves . . .
(Hysterical laughter.)

MARCO BONE
He calls Volonty, the high-wire artist who asked all those
questions. They used her body, and there was plenty more all
unused. Now she's Houdini's best detective. Ask him why.

HOUDINI

She has gone among the mediums, into their dark rooms and she knows their shabby tricks. She's my right-hand woman and a crack detective.

VOLONTY

I am here because I consider it my duty. We have laws against cholera, yellow fever, and smallpox. Why is there no law against this contamination by which frauds have bamboozled prominent politicians and scientists ... which is an easy thing to do.

HOUDINI

Thank you, Volonty.

VARICK

How is it easy?

VOLONTY

They are gentlemen, sir. They come to a séance, they would not touch a medium when she comes dressed as a man, or a man dressed as a woman. Their theories are in their mind, they would not touch anything. How are you going to find out anything if you don't touch it, isn't it so, Harry?

HOUDINI

She's my best detective.

VOLONTY

(*In a poster pose.*)
I feel for the truth.
(*Response from the audience.*)

VARICK

What holds back the body will confine the mind.

VOLONTY

How can you prove that you don't have those powers?

HOUDINI

Oh, come on. *I* go through a keyhole?

VOLONTY

They claim that you dematerialize your body, ooze through, and put yourself together again. How do you do it?

HOUDINI

I can take hold of the rational and irrational; I can use my one gift; I can speak out against lies, like anyone else. We are all born alike.

CONGRESSMAN

I don't follow this! It's all a plot of the Jews!

SPECTATOR

He wrote a letter to the Pope. I saw a copy.

SECOND SPECTATOR

Maybe he's secretly a Catholic.

MARCO BONE

I don't think this is good for your career, Harry. Or your marriage.

HOUDINI
You willing to testify, Marco?

MARCO BONE
Sure, but don't be self-destructive.

VOLONTY
Protecting the magician, now and forever.

MARCO BONE
Protecting him from himself is what I'm for.
What are you for, honey?

VOLONTY *(Song: "Ecstasy of a Woman Detective")*
I LOVE USING WHAT I'VE GOT
LOVE NOT BEING WHAT I'M NOT —
AFTER A LONG TIME OF ONE KIND OF LIVING,
AND IT WAS ALL RIGHT, IT WAS REALLY PARTLY GOOD,
FULL OF ONE-SIDE OF THINGS,
AND DISTURBING . . . AND ABSORBING . . . ALMOST
    EVERY DAY . . .
BUT
THEN THE NEW LIFE CAME ALONG, BRINGING
THE JOY OF REACHING, OF STRETCHING, OF BEING
    EFFECTIVE —
THIS IS ANOTHER PLACE, THIS IS ANOTHER WAY,
THE ECSTASY OF A WOMAN DETECTIVE —
AND WHAT I DETECT, WHAT I REALLY FIND
IS YOUR BODY-AND-MIND AND YOUR LIFE AND MY
    LIFE AND
            MY BODY-AND-MIND;

THE JOY OF BEING ME, A DETECTIVE,
THE JOY OF THINKING NEW, LIKE BEING
   UNBELIEVABLY BARE,
FINDING SOMETHING OF MYSELF THAT HAS NEVER
   BEEN AWARE —
THE ECSTASY OF FEELING FOR WHAT'S THERE!

MARCO BONE

Those targets are really moving. You can detect . . . you can expose . . . can you duplicate?

VOLONTY

That's for me to know, you to find out.

HOUDINI

(Calls him to testify.)
You've known me for . . .

MARCO BONE

All your professional life.

HOUDINI

In the jails, under the ice, with the circuses, where I ran séances myself in the tank towns — all "fixed" —

MARCO BONE

I heard the newsboys yell that you died in the river. I saw you when the phone rang. Anybody can tell fortunes, but —

HOUDINI

And, in your opinion . . .

MARCO BONE

You do things I cannot understand. You have a gift, and you make your gift to us. Maybe you don't understand it yourself . . .
(To the chamber.)
This is a great man.
(Uproar.)

VARICK

Any further disturbance, and I'll clear the chamber.

MARCO BONE

(Carried away by his own talk.)
He performs extraordinary escapes. He can talk to the dead. He calls it duplicating, but I say it's supernatural. He just does it, it's a form of saying it to us. He can mystify the wisest judge and the believing child. I have seen their eyes.

HOUDINI

Marco! I'm trying to tell the truth!

MARCO BONE

Well. This isn't a trial. I'm telling what I see.

CONGRESSMAN

Have *him* up on trial!

MARCO BONE

Open your eyes, Harry. Admit everything.
They want to hear it.
(Steps down.)

VOLONTY

Marco, what have you done?

MARCO BONE

He's a magician, why should he turn and face them?

VOLONTY

The American hero as escape artist. He's escaped escape.

MARCO BONE

No, he's just standing, speaking for what he is.
You know, they'll probably put me away.

VOLONTY

You cut through everything! Your loyal neck, and your damn
fool chin! I'll wait for you, Marco.

CONGRESSMAN

Well, what do you do?

HOUDINI

Say you watch a bullfighter. You're fascinated. You're the
bull. You stare, you hardly move your eyes. All those wounds
in your back! All you see is a huge red cape . . .
(*An enormous red area opens on the back curtain.*)
. . . and a point of light.
(*Intense spot of light beside the red.*)
But *that* is the sword point that will kill you.
(*From now on,* SPECTATORS *crowd him; sinister, continual
movement.*)

CONGRESSMAN

Stand back, please, you photographers! *Will you stand back!*

MARCO BONE

I am back at the shooting gallery.
Volonty goes on, hunting. Who's she after?
Read your newspaper.

ENSEMBLE

Do you attack faith?

HOUDINI

Our emotions are part of our bodies and ourselves.

ENSEMBLE

How do you juggle? How do you escape?

HOUDINI

I don't call it religion. Here, here's a trumpet.
(Gives the trumpet to VARICK.*)*
Say, "Hello, kind spirit."
(Music begins.)

VARICK

I don't hear anything.

HOUDINI

You must have faith. That's what they say.

VARICK

Now I hear something . . . Oh, for God's sake!
(Throws the trumpet down and laughs. An OLD WOMAN
comes forward; some reminder of CECILIA.*)*

141

OLD WOMAN

Did you destroy yourself, Houdini?
(She laughs softly.)
My dead do live. They are in my life, each day speaks. I don't talk about communication any more.

HOUDINI

Thank you.

ENSEMBLE

He's crazy! He's brutal, he torments his wife, he's unspeakable.
(Great roar of voices, music.)

HOUDINI

My character is under attack.
My last witness, Mrs. Houdini.
(She takes the stand. He acts as questioner. It becomes personal now, completely.)
Step this way, Mrs. Houdini.
They say I hypnotize you, that I'm vile to you.
(Chains in the air.)
Have I ever been crazy, unless it was about you?

BEATRICE

(Chooses to say.)
No.

ENSEMBLE

Shame, Houdini. He's a fake. He's insane.
Get him!
He's against visions! Clown! Butcher! Whip!

HOUDINI

The transformation took place in a storm of light, not in a dark, filthy room with hands groping for you, for money. *(Shakes them off. Stands there, at the beginning of a new phase.)*

ENSEMBLE

Ask him about the chains! Ask him about the jails!
You know that burial plot? You know that paper she signed?
Suppose it doesn't work out like that?
(BEATRICE and HOUDINI embrace. None of these attacks reach him, now that he has made his stand and stopped escaping.)

BEATRICE

None of it can touch you, now that you make your stand. *(Black out. Change of scene.)*

MARCO BONE

Now the three medical students are walking down the avenue in the rain. The rainy lights. They are very near the theater where Houdini is. A piece of apparatus has fallen on his ankle. The bone is cracked. He is in pain.
(A theater. HOUDINI's dressing room. HOUDINI and BESS. HOUDINI is lying on a couch, his trouser leg pulled up. BESS is massaging his ankle.)

BEATRICE

Your fine ankle, Harry. Like a racehorse. Here?

HOUDINI

Your hands are marvelous.

143

BEATRICE
It's broken. Don't do the show.

HOUDINI
Come on, it's almost healed. A crack, anyway.
(*She massages the ankle in silence. Now she is bandaging it again.*)

BEATRICE
Sometimes I think that dog's my child, Harry.

HOUDINI
Sometimes I think what mother was going to say was "be your own child." How can that be?

BEATRICE
You know, whenever we come to this river, I see you beneath the ice.

HOUDINI
And what do you do?
(*A knock at the door.*)

BEATRICE
You're not expecting anyone?

HOUDINI
Just a minute . . . the young fellow with the drawing.
(*He pulls down his trouser leg. She goes to the door and opens it to the* THREE MEDICAL STUDENTS.)

SECOND MEDICAL STUDENT
This isn't a good time for you—

HOUDINI

Of course it is. Come in. And your friends.
(They come in.)

SECOND MEDICAL STUDENT

Thank you for your kindness. I just thought the eyes —
(Shows the portrait to BEATRICE. *The portrait appears on the
back wall.)*
I can see.

BEATRICE

Yes, perhaps the eyes. And Houdini will rest.

HOUDINI

(This brings him up, standing.)
Five minutes, and then I dress for my act.

SECOND MEDICAL STUDENT

You have the most extraordinary eyes I've ever seen.

THIRD MEDICAL STUDENT

Is that how you hypnotize them?

HOUDINI

The reaches of being? That what you care about?

THIRD MEDICAL STUDENT

I'm those reaches. Sleeping with the lights on, memorizing
those nerves, those nerves —

HOUDINI

But those are marvelous times. When you come to the end of
exhaustion and walk out the other side — swim out the other

side. When you come to the end of belief and disbelief, and find yourself in a place where everything is lit with another light — touch something beyond touch —

THIRD MEDICAL STUDENT
But all you have to do is entertain them.

BEATRICE
No, he's a different fish altogether.

THIRD MEDICAL STUDENT
Draw those eyes, Tony! Sharpened on darkness with his wife there all the time . . .
(Smacks his fist into his own hand.)
. . . in bed with him every day and every night!

HOUDINI
(Laughs.)
And the discipline, too, all your life long!

THIRD MEDICAL STUDENT
We train for epidemics, staying awake for five days. And you: another town, another hotel?

BEATRICE
No. He's challenged everybody.

THIRD MEDICAL STUDENT
I've seen those challenges. Fake me, someone. Hit me anyone, anytime.

BEATRICE

(In a burst that parallels her burst at the end of ACT ONE.*)*
He's the man on fire who walks out alive. He's the rider of
the death comet. He held out against them in the hearing,
called them Fraud when they tried to take his profession
away from him by chopping him down with attacks and
slobbering hate. Stood against them when they called him
Mystic, although, I don't know, I don't know, he's a cascade
of powers —
*(Sees him staring at her, he is finally filled with her praise,
something in him being spoken to that had never been
reached.)*
They don't know, they don't know, these boys like memory-
machines, how could they know your fighting, diving body
and your life, full of power, full of sex, full of belief.
(While he is fixed on what she is doing, HOUDINI *is hit full
force in the stomach by the* THIRD MEDICAL STUDENT.*)*

THIRD MEDICAL STUDENT

(The first blow was to the solar plexus.)
What do —
You want us —
To believe?
(Three sharp blows. HOUDINI *collapses on the couch. The
other two students pull the third one away. Men burst in; the
students leave.)*

HOUDINI

I'm all right.
Bess, the whole thing is turning.

147

Hold me!
(Spin of color and music. Another dressing room.)
Give her some champagne.
(VOLONTY *is with* BEATRICE, *pouring a drink.* MARCO BONE *guards the door.)*
No, not for me. I'm at another lock.

MARCO BONE
The doctor's just outside, Harry.

HOUDINI
There's no cure.
(Changes his tone.)
I'll walk out of this one, whether the locks give or not.

BEATRICE
Stay, Harry. A little longer.

HOUDINI
Bess. I want to promise you something. I'll come back to you. I'll make a way. I'll come back.

BEATRICE
I'll bring your audience, Harry, I'll be there. But for myself—I won't try to come back.

HOUDINI
Pain. Fire. Promises.
(He dies. They crowd around.)

VOLONTY
—He's gone. Dead, disappeared. Illuminated man.

MARCO BONE

I am back at the shooting gallery.

Volonty goes on, hunting. Who's she after?

Read your newspaper. The law against fortune-tellers? Of course, it did *not* go through. Tell your fortune, ladies and gentlemen? What are all his escapes for? What did he make his stand for? Go further, you say? Does Houdini go further? Breaking out forever?

Beatrice waits for the word from Harry.

(BEATRICE, *coming out of her destruction to concentrate on getting his message, drinking, waiting, almost as she was when she waited for him to come out of the river. But something does come, a message in the form of a song.*)

HOUDINI   (*Song: "Let Me See, Let Me Feel"*)

LET ME SEE, LET ME FEEL,

LET ME KNOW WHAT IS REAL,

LET ME BELIEVE —

(*As* HOUDINI *sang it when he spilled the acid.*

Music and colors around BEATRICE. *Snatches of song-music roaring past, River Music. Long pink flashes, going blue-green and black at last.* BEATRICE *drinks. The voices deny.*)

ENSEMBLE

—False.

—She told me about that song last week. Sure I passed it on.

—Listen, she gave an interview six months ago, and told about "Let me see, let me feel—"

—I saw it in print.

If you believe that, you'll believe anything.

It didn't even sound like his voice.

(Singing, crowing, laughing, a chaos of noise. HOUDINI *steps out of the blackness to the point closest to the audience.)*

HOUDINI
Incredible! But I believe the incredible,
Swallow anything, eat the inedible,
Convince Missouri, bamboozle the Dutch.
And I make, I make, by touch, by touch.
Great touch by which we do all things,
Even our imaginings.
Even numbers, even words —
"They touched me," we have heard.
That's, you know, "They opened me."
Open yourself, for we are locks,
Open each other, we are keys.
Then, if you are touched by these,
Our people who reached out to you,
Touch yourself and your neighbor, too,
Make by touch as man made you —
Touch yourself as I touch myself
        Touching man
        And woman too.
(Gently claps his hands together and stretches them out.)

THE END

ABOUT PARIS PRESS

Paris Press is a young nonprofit press publishing work by ground-breaking women writers that has been neglected or misrepresented by the literary world. Publishing one to two books a year, Paris Press values work that is daring in style and in its courage to speak truthfully about society, culture, history, and the human heart. To publish our books, Paris Press relies on support from organizations and individuals. Please help Paris Press keep the voices of essential women writers in print and known. All contributions are tax-deductible.

Cover and text design by Ivan Holmes.
Typesetting by R&S Book Composition.
Text in Stempel Garamond.
Printed by Quebecor World.
Cover art reproduced with permission from Sidney H. Radner.